Becoming a True *Worshipper*

Timothy D. Lucas Sr.

Becoming a True Worshipper
by *Timothy D. Lucas Sr.*

Signalman Publishing
www.signalmanpublishing.com
email: info@signalmanpublishing.com
Kissimmee, Florida

© Copyright 2013 Timothy D. Lucas Sr. All rights reserved. No portion of this book may be reproduced by any means, electronic or mechanical, including photocopying, recording, or by any information storage retrieval system, without permission of the copyright's owner, except for the inclusion of brief quotations for a review.

ISBN: 978-1-935991-96-0

Library of Congress Control Number: 2013936594

Unless otherwise indicated, Bible quotations are taken from The King James Version (KJV) of the Holy Bible.

Scripture quotations noted NIV are from the HOLY BIBLE: NEW INTERNATIONL VERSION®. Copyright © 1973, 1978, 1984 by International Bible Society. Used by permission of Zondervan Publishing House. All rights reserved

Scripture quotations noted NKJV are from THE NEW KING JAMES VERSION. Copyright © 1979,1980,1982,1990, 1994 by Thomas Nelson, Inc.

Scripture quotations noted AMP are taken from the Amplified® Bible, Copyright © 1954, 1958, 1962, 1964, 1965, 1987 by The Lockman Foundation. Used by permission. (www.Lockman.org).

ver_1_2014

Signalman Publishing

In Dedication

To the love of my life, my beautiful wife Rochelle, for your endless love and support. You are the best! To my children (Mia, Kimyata, Cherelle, & Tim Jr.) and grandchildren (Jamari & Prince) who are destined to do great things for the Kingdom of God. To my Mother (Ida) and Father (Arthur) for unselfishly sowing into my life. To my sisters (Valerie & Adrean) and brothers (Ulysess, Kelvin & Tyrone) for all of the good times and the bad times throughout the years. To all of my spiritual leaders and mentors who have provoked me to operate with integrity and in excellence. To my church family (KOMI-Virginia) who are steadfast in the faith and committed to becoming True Worshippers.

Contents

Foreword 6
Introduction 12
1: Created for Worship 15
2: The Corporate Worship Experience 24
3: The Character of a True Worshipper 35
4: The Fall of Lucifer .49
5: The Battle for Your Worship 58
6: Worship is a Weapon 71
7: Ministering Through Adversities 77
8: Seasons - Waiting on God 89
9: A Lifestyle of Worship 98
10: The Heart of a Servant 106
11: Preparing the Way for Your Ministry 114
Conclusion 120

Foreword

Greetings, and Shalom.

My name is Joseph W. King, the Founder, Apostle, and Senior Pastor of Kingdom Outreach Ministries International, (KOMI), Okinawa Japan, the base from where my wife, Pastor Kimberly Ann King and I minister. The ministry of KOMI includes three additional church plants: Kingdom Outreach Ministries International (Dumfries, VA), pastored by Timothy D. Lucas (author of this book) and his wife Rochelle; Judah Sunrise Ministries (Yaka Village, Okinawa, Japan), pastored by Vincent Smith and wife Valicia (Lady-V), and thirdly, Zebulun Christian Outreach Center (Village of Henoko, Nago City, Okinawa, Japan), pastored by Dominic Guerra and his wife Sandy. I have been in ministry for seventeen years and pastoring/pioneering for thirteen years. We are currently working to lay foundation to an apostolic and prophetic council and network that will be the base for connecting with and providing oversight to ministries throughout the USA. I can truly say that it all connects back to my relationship and time spent with the author, Pastor Timothy D. Lucas. As you break the seal on this book and devour its content, you will grasp that Timothy is a student of the Word. A true worshiper at heart, he possesses an apostolic anointing and, as King

David, has a passion to restore true worship to the house of God. As a priest of the Lord, he knows how to handle the Ark! He knows how to set the atmosphere, how to usher in the presence of God, how to shift with the move of God, and what to do when the shekinah shows up.

As such, it is my hope that you will be captivated, educated, blessed, and inspired to engage or enter into the next dimension of your worship experience with the Father by reading this book. For that should be our greatest desire, to worship the Lord our God in Spirit and in Truth. Believe me, there are different levels of worship. As you glean from the writings of my son in the ministry, Pastor Timothy D. Lucas, you will connect with a dynamic and true worshiper who loves the Lord and lives what he ministers.

Our relationship started in Okinawa, Japan thirteen years ago while we both were on active duty in the Marine Corps. During two tours of duty in Okinawa, Pastor Lucas was my assistant pastor, minister of music, and main worship leader. Nearing the close of his career in the Corps, Pastor Kim and I sent Pastor Lucas to Virginia where we planted Kingdom Outreach Ministries International in the city of Quantico.. We installed him there to pastor and oversee a new work of ministry helping to fulfill the vision of, "Reaching a Diverse Community – Perfecting the Saints – Impacting the World." I trust him and the anointing of God upon his life to do great exploits for the Kingdom. He is a good son, faithful husband and father, mighty man of God, intercessor and prayer warrior, dynamic psalmist, worship leader, and he is full of wisdom and of the Holy Ghost. Timothy was also my armor bearer during a season where he was sought after by several ministries due to the manifold gifts of God he operated in, yet he remained "faithful" to his God given assignment to assist me in pushing the vision for KOMI. Because of his faithfulness and focus responding with obedience to God, a foundation was laid for God to bless him richly, bring manifestation of his vision, and launch ministry through him. He was my Joshua to Moses and my Timothy to Paul.

If you are a true worshiper or desire to become one, this book is for you! It will minister to many by increasing their knowledge and understanding of what true worship is. It will also set others free from a spirit of religious and traditional bondage that may have held them captive to unbiblical precepts, concepts, and principles preventing them from experiencing the best worship—true worship!

In this book, Pastor Lucas addresses such topics as: You were Created to Worship; The Corporate Worship Experience; Character of a True Worshiper; Fighting for Your Worship; Worship as a Weapon, A Lifestyle of Worship, and many more. It's a great read both for the new believer and to the experienced and mature disciples.

Allow this book to infuse you with revelation from God's throne room to gain deeper access into His presence where the shekinah glory rests upon you to impart what you need from Jehovah (healing, deliverance, restoration, strength, new joys, vision, re-vision, refreshing, and so much more). Praise and worship is also a *key* to facing the challenges of life. It is not only a key when entering challenges, it's the way through and the way out. It is also the way to respond to God after He has brought you out of life's challenging experience.

Many people think you can receive power from the Word of God through "osmosis." However, the Word of God commands us to *study* to show ourselves approved of God (2 Tim 2:15). You can't get revelation and the power of God's Word by just looking at, sitting near, or just dreaming about it. God said He rewards those who not only believe in Him, but also diligently seek Him (Heb 1:6). Therefore, you will be blessed by embracing the principles and concepts of praise and worship contained in this book.

Worship activates God to provide for and move on your behalf as you dwell in the secret place of the Most High God and abide under the shadow of the almighty (Psalm 91:1). God will cover you! Get into His presence and allow "El-Shaddai," the Self Sufficient and Almighty One, to break forth and minister on your behalf. He is watching and waiting to perform His Word (Jeremiah 1:12)!

The Word of God makes it clear that we have been brought out of the darkness and into this marvelous light so that we can *show forth* His praise (1Peter 2:9)! That means by way of willful expression verbally, physically, mentally, and spiritually. There should be a "showing," first of all because the divine connection with God causes us to respond in worship with or without someone leading us. Secondly, God wants the world to "see" His glory through us so that the world also may draw nigh to Him. I believe when the world sees us give praises in spite of our situations and the pressures of life, they too will begin to give glory to God (Matt 5:16) and possibly come to have an experience like Cornelius had in his house, (Acts 10:25-48), resulting in the salvation of his whole family.

God is a Spirit, and they that worship Him *must* worship Him in spirit and in truth (John 4:23-24)! Are you a true worshiper? Do you know the truth about worship? I thought I did until I met Timothy. Although I was his pastor and spiritual father in the ministry, I learned much about praise and worship from him. It is the anointing upon his life, and it's the anointing that broke the yoke of religion and tradition from my neck. It removed the burden of my insecurities about God, ministry and its vision. Yes, as a pastor, I still had personal insecurities that were hidden. If kept there, they may have been exposed sooner or later, but the GRACE of God kept me and covered me, and the anointing of God through Pastor Lucas' ministry gifts set me free.

I want to remind you that if you are a true worshiper or desire to be one, this book is for you! Buy it, read it, meditate on it and watch the Spirit of God unveil truth, wisdom, knowledge, and power as you worship not only from zeal and feelings, but from revelation of how to and why you must worship in spirit and in truth. I write this foreword because I know from experience that the author is an usher assigned to lead us to the throne of the almighty.

Well, don't just look at this book and hope for osmosis to occur from its contents. Buy it, read it, and meditate on it along with the scriptures herein. It will empower you to *Become a True Worshiper* too.

Joseph W. King
Founder, Apostle, and Senior Pastor
Kingdom Outreach Ministries International
www.komi-okinawa.com

Introduction

> But the hour cometh, and now is, when the true worshippers shall worship the Father in spirit and in truth: for the Father seeketh such to worship him. God is a Spirit: and they that worship him must worship him in spirit and in truth. (John 4: 23-24)

One of the most valued freedoms that an individual can have is the freedom to Worship as they please. In our society today, there are various forms of worship, several postures of worship, and even more places of worship. There are thousands of religions and denominations in the world and each has an interpretation of what it means to worship. As Christians, the Holy Bible should be our main source of information and inspiration concerning worship. In the scriptures, we see countless examples of men and women engaged in some form of worship. Abraham worshipped God. King David worshipped God. Yes, even Jesus Christ was a worshipper.

Worship is more than just a religious service or the gathering of a congregation. It is not restricted to singing songs, lifting our hands, waving flags, chanting, or kneeling and praying. True Worship can include these aforementioned postures of worship, but there is much more. Jesus said, "…God is a Spirit, and they that worship him must worship him in spirit and in truth." This leads me to believe that there is more to worship than an outward expression or physical posture.

Worship is something that Jesus obviously wants us to get a clear understanding of. It is important to him because it is important to God. God loves True Worshippers. He loves them so much that He is "seeking" for them. God is looking for believers who are going to go beyond surface level worship and truly touch His heart. It is my desire over the next few chapters to expand our concept of worship and help us to understand how to become a True Worshipper.

1

Created for Worship

Bible scholars, theologians, authors, preachers and teachers have been debating over the purpose of man's creation for years. Everyone seems to have his or her opinion as to why we (humans) were created. In all honesty, I believe that there are several reasons for our existence here on earth. For the purposes of this book, we are focusing on one of the many reasons why we were created; and that is to Worship God.

There are certain attributes about God that are exclusive to Him. God is Omniscient, which means that He is "all knowing". There is nothing beyond God's sphere of knowledge. He knows every intricate detail of everything that exists in this world. God is also Omnipresent, which means "all-present". God is everywhere at the same time. It is also important to note that God's Omnipresence is not limited to geographical boundaries. He exists in every aspect of time to include the past, the present and in the future. Now, you may be asking yourself, "How can God still be in the past?" Well, God is not restricted to time boundaries like we are. He has exclusive liberties that we don't have. God is not in time, but He is the Father of time. Another attribute of God is that He is Omnipotent, which means "all powerful". He is self-existent and eternal. There was no need for anyone to create God because He always has been God, and will always be. The Bible says in **Genesis 1:1**, "In the beginning God created the heaven and the earth." Another reference to the creative power of God can be found in John 1:1-3:

> In the beginning was the Word, and the Word was with God, and the Word was God. ²The same was in the beginning with God. ³<u>All things were made by him</u>; and without him was not any thing made that was made.

The Bible clearly states that God made all things. Not only did God create heaven and earth, but also everything within them. God created man in his image and placed us here on earth to live. We can physically see most of God's creation such as the mountains, rivers, lakes, trees, animals, plants, etc. But there is also the heavenly realm that most of us have never seen. There have been some people that God has allowed a glimpse into heaven by way of dreams, visions, etc. (i.e. God allowed John to visit His majestic kingdom and instructed him to write the book of Revelation, which contains graphic details about the appearance and activities in Heaven). However, most believers have never had this type of divine experience. For the majority, the best images that we can ascribe to heaven come from descriptions in the Bible. Let's take a look at the scriptures and note how things are done in Heaven.

> Praise ye the LORD. Praise ye the LORD from the heavens: praise him in the heights. ²Praise ye him, all his angels: praise ye him, all his hosts. ³Praise ye him, sun and moon: praise him, all ye stars of light. ⁴Praise him, ye heavens of heavens, and ye waters that *be* above the heavens. ⁵Let them praise the name of the LORD: for he commanded, and they were created. ⁶He hath also stablished them forever and ever: he hath made a decree which shall not pass. (Psalm 148:1-6)

We can note from the scriptures that the entire host of heaven is commanded to praise God. None of the heavenly beings are exempt from lifting up the name of the Lord Jesus. It is also amazing to see that the sun, moon and stars are commanded to praise the Lord! Another picture of worship in heaven can be seen in the book of Isaiah:

> In the year that king Uzziah died I saw also the Lord sitting upon a throne, high and lifted up, and his train filled the temple. ²Above it stood the seraphims: each one had six wings; with twain he covered his face, and with twain he covered his feet, and with twain he did fly. ³And one cried unto another, and said, Holy, holy, holy, *is*

> the LORD of hosts: the whole earth *is* full of his glory. [4]And the posts of the door moved at the voice of him that cried, and the house was filled with smoke. [5]Then said I, Woe *is* me! for I am undone; because I *am* a man of unclean lips, and I dwell in the midst of a people of unclean lips: for mine eyes have seen the King, the LORD of hosts. (Isaiah 6:1-5)

We can see that there are angels that are continuously offering up praise and worship unto God. They have an obligation to carry out the commands of God, but even then they are displaying an attitude of worship. Obedience to the commandments of God is one of the truest postures of worship. It displays not only a form (or method) of worship, but also a character of worship. God designed the angels to be perfect in character; which overflowed into their worship and created the perfect environment for His glory to dwell. Based on the scriptures, I think that it would be a good assumption that the angels of the Lord are indeed True Worshippers. So what about man? Are we required to worship God like the angels? Let's see what the Bible has to say about us.

> And Abraham said unto his young men, Abide ye here with the ass; and I and the lad will go yonder and worship, and come again to you. [6]And Abraham took the wood of the burnt

> offering, and laid it upon Isaac his son; and he took the fire in his hand, and a knife; and they went both of them together. ⁷And Isaac spake unto Abraham his father, and said, My father: and he said, Here am I, my son. And he said, Behold the fire and the wood: but where is the lamb for a burnt offering? ⁸And Abraham said, My son, God will provide himself a lamb for a burnt offering: so they went both of them together. (Genesis 22: 5-8)

There is a school of thought among Bible scholars, which simply implies that the very first time any important word (or principle) is mentioned in the Bible, it gives that word its most complete, and accurate, meaning. It not only serves as a "key" in understanding the word's Biblical concept, but to also provide a foundation for its fuller development in later parts of the Bible. Genesis 2:5 is the first time the word **Worship** is mentioned in the Bible. To get a clear understanding of this passage of scripture we need some background information.

Abraham was an honorable and righteous man. He was already very old and his wife was beyond childbearing years. God had promised Abraham that He would give him a son and that he would be the "…father of many nations." Abraham believed that God would do what He said. Although it took many years, Abraham trusted God and eventually Isaac was born. After a few years, Abraham was challenged by God to offer Isaac as a sacrifice.

> And he said, Take now thy son, thine only *son* Isaac, whom thou lovest, and get thee into the land of Moriah; and offer him there for a burnt offering upon one of the mountains which I will tell thee of. (Genesis 22:2)

This means that God was asking him to kill his son. Can you imagine the challenge facing Abraham? Isaac was the son of his old age. He was the long awaited answer to Abraham's prayer. Now God was asking him to give up the very thing that he treasured the most. For Abraham to go through with this act there would have to be an act of obedience, sacrifice and faith (expectation):

Obedience: This required him to do something that he wouldn't normally do. A father would not normally agree to slay his only son just because he heard a voice in his head. This tells me that Abraham must have truly had a relationship with God and that he clearly recognized the voice of God. He was willing to obey God even when it didn't make sense to his natural mind. He exercised one of the greatest forms of worship; and that is extreme obedience.

Sacrifice: This required him to give up something that meant something to him. Isaac was the pride of Abraham's life. Imagine how he felt walking through the villages and market places with his son by his side. There is no doubt that he had big plans for his son. Isaac represented his future and the future of generations to come. However, Abraham was willing to give up everything to please God. He trusted that God would perform his Word in spite of any situation or circumstance. He didn't allow his personal feelings, wants or desires to interfere with his relationship with God. He removed all barriers that was hindering him from worshipping God with all that he had.

Faith: Abraham knew that God had made him a promise concerning his seed. He knew in his heart that God had already thought this thing through. Abraham believed God! Even if he would have to go through with this unthinkable act, Abraham knew that God was able to perform a miracle to see his promises fulfilled. Abraham worshipped God in his actions by trusting God even in the midst of trying circumstances. The Bible tells us that it is impossible to please God without faith. Our faith pleases God, thus can be a form of worship.

> And [so] the Scripture was fulfilled that says, Abraham believed in (adhered to, trusted in, and relied on) God, and this was accounted to him as righteousness (as conformity to God's will in thought and deed), and he was called God's friend. (James 2: 23 AMP)

We must understand that God desires a relationship with us. We must also know that our level of worship is predicated upon our level of relationship that we have with God. This act of obedience by Abraham also demonstrated patience and perseverance. It was a three-day journey from where they lived to the place that God commanded them to go for the sacrificial offering. As we strive to become True Worshippers, there are times when we will have to persevere. Specifically, in a corporate worship setting, we must understand that sometimes we have to press in during our times of praise and worship. There are times where we will have to wait on the Lord to get our breakthrough. God doesn't always manifest Himself instantly, but like Abraham we must go to the place of worship and wait on the Lord.

As we think about this story, Abraham and Isaac *went together to the place of worship*. There had to be an act of obedience on behalf of Abraham and Isaac. If we were to look at this as it pertains to the Church, Abraham represented the leadership (i.e. Pastor, Worship Leader, Praise Leader, etc,). Abraham knew, saw and heard more than Isaac. He received direct instructions from God. Isaac represented the congregation/followers. Neither understood all that was happening, but they were both submissive and receptive to God. Once it was evident that they both were submitted, the Lord came in and provided what was needed. With God's presence comes the blessing (deliverance and substance).

> And Abraham called the name of that place **Jehovahjireh**: as it is said to this day, In the mount of the LORD it shall be seen. (Genesis 22:14 KJV)

> And Abraham said unto his young men, Abide ye here with the ass; ***and I and the lad will go yonder and worship***, and come again to you. (Genesis 22:5)

As we look at these passages of scripture, we can see that there is more to worship than just singing a few songs, lifting our hands and getting emotional. We identified that there were acts of obedience, faith, sacrifice, submission, respect/reverence, compliance, agreement, and devotion. Becoming a True Worshiper will require a total surrender to God (Heart, mind, body and soul).

> God is a Spirit: and they that worship him must worship him in spirit and in truth. (John 4:24)

In the story of Abraham, we can see that there was a progression that took place. It was Abraham's Praise that got him to a place of Worship!

PRAISE led to WORSHIP

Positioned to hear the voice of God

Recognized the voice of God

Acted on God's word in faith

Individual physical response to the Word (obedience)

Sacrifice made

Enjoyed the presence and blessing (provision) of the Lord

2

The Corporate Worship Experience

Every Sunday morning, people of various denominations, backgrounds, races, ages, and social classes gather to participate in the corporate worship services. Most people call this, "going to worship" or "going to church." This is where Christians can fellowship together, sing praises unto the Lord, hear the preached Word of God, and give their tithes and offering. Every aspect of the worship service is very important and has a purpose. This includes everything from the parking attendant to the pastor preaching the Word. All of these activities are a part of the *corporate worship experience*.

As True Worshippers, we are partially responsible for preparing the spiritual atmosphere in our places of worship. We should be monitoring and observing every aspect of the worship service to ensure that the atmosphere is set for a divine visitation. God is looking to save a lost soul, so everyone has a part to play in ensuring that nothing distracts the unbeliever from receiving what God has prepared for them during that corporate worship service.

There is a tendency to think that worship begins when the Worship Team gets up and starts singing. This is not an accurate assessment. God can touch an individual's heart at any point of the service. Everyone is responsible for ushering the presence of the Lord during the worship service. True Worshippers are a very important element in the corporate worship experience. Because we have been displaying a *character of worship* all week, this will overflow into our worship settings. We will be walking in unity and in tune with the Holy Spirit. This will make it easier for the Lord to have His way during the service.

We know that the Bible says in John 4:24, "God is a Spirit: and they that <u>worship</u> him must worship him in spirit and in truth." We don't want to spend our lives going through routines and rituals that don't line up with God's definition of "True Worship." Our desire and our passion should be to love the Lord with all of our hearts, our souls and our minds.

> Master, which is the great commandment in the law? [37]Jesus said unto him, Thou shalt love the Lord thy God with all thy heart, and with all thy soul, and with all thy mind. [38]This is the first and great commandment. (Matthew 22: 36-38, KJV)

To love God is to obey Him. This is why we are striving to learn how to properly and reverently approach God's throne in worship. We want to worship Him in a way that is pleasing in His sight.

In our last chapter, we mentioned Abraham and the commitment that he had toward God. We identified events that were taking place the first time the word "Worship" was mentioned in the Bible. Abraham demonstrated an act of Obedience, Sacrifice and Faith as he postured himself to worship God. Let's now take a look at some of the patterns of worship demonstrated in the Old Testament. Although the Law of Moses no longer binds us, we must understand that God gave us a pattern for our learning.

> And David called for Zadok and Abiathar the priests, and for the Levites, for Uriel, Asaiah, and Joel, Shemaiah, and Eliel, and Amminadab, [12]And said to them, You are the heads of the fathers' houses of the Levites; sanctify yourselves, both you and your brethren, that you may bring up the ark of the Lord, the God of Israel, to the place that I have prepared for it. [13]For because you bore it not [as God directed] at the first, the Lord our God broke forth upon us—*because we did not seek Him in the way He ordained.* (1 Chronicles 15:11-13)

In the early days, God gave instructions to Moses concerning the tabernacle (tent). The Tabernacle was to be a representative dwelling place for God. God was very specific when he designed the tabernacle. He was specific about which items would go into the tabernacle. He was specific about who could perform certain activities in the tabernacle. One of these activities was the handling of the Ark of the Covenant. The Ark of the Covenant represented the Presence and the Glory of the Lord. Ultimately, this is why we worship. We want to be in the Presence and the Glory of the Lord. The Tabernacle represented a dwelling place for God. It was the place where the people went to meet with God!

There are many people that believe that you do not have to come to church to have an experience with God. While this is true, God has established the church for a purpose.

> And let us consider one another in order to stir up love and good works, [25]not forsaking the assembling of ourselves together, as *is* the manner of some, but exhorting *one another*, and so much the more as you see the Day approaching. (Hebrews 10: 24-26, NKJV)

There are some things that you will get from a corporate worship experience that you can't get on your own. As we prepare to go into God's presence, we can exhort each other, we can encourage each other, we can celebrate together, we can testify, we can embrace, we can touch and agree, etc. We can put more demons to flight corporately than we could ever do individually.

> Let the word of Christ dwell in you richly in all wisdom, teaching and admonishing one another in psalms and hymns and spiritual songs, singing with grace in your hearts to the Lord. (Colossians 3:16, NKJV)

You cannot separate worship from the Word of God. To worship God in Spirit and in Truth, you have to be in line with the Word of God. We are to teach "one another" which indicates that we are not just to do this thing by ourselves. A part of being a true worshiper is the verbal declarations from our mouths. This indicates that there should be an active participation in the corporate worship service. This scripture describes three ways we can do this.

- **Psalms** – This is simply singing the scriptures. This doesn't require an eloquent voice or even any vocal ability. This is just making up your own tune as you "sing" the scriptures. There are 150 Psalms in the Bible, but we don't have to limit our Psalms to those. We can sing any scripture back to God. We can sing scriptures to each other that will be a word of encouragement.

- **Hymns** – These are songs that have been written by someone else. This includes those songs that have been published in hymnals, but are not limited to those hymn books. A hymn is simply a song or ode in praise or honor of God. We are encouraged to sing hymns when we gather together in our corporate worship services.

- **Spiritual Songs** – These are songs that are birthed from within our spirits. They are not on CD, or written down, not recorded, or copy written. These are songs that you sing to the Lord as they come to you. They may not rhyme, they may not make sense to anyone else but you, they might not be in tune, but they are spiritual songs. These are songs that touch the heart of God. They are straight from your heart to His. Let's take another look at 1 Chronicles 15.

> And David called for Zadok and Abiathar the priests, and for the Levites, for Uriel, Asaiah, and Joel, Shemaiah, and Eliel, and Amminadab, [12]And said to them, You are the heads of the fathers' houses of the Levites; sanctify yourselves, both you and your brethren, that you may bring up the ark of the Lord, the God of Israel, to the place that I have prepared for it. [13]For because you bore it not [as God directed] at the first, the Lord our God broke forth upon us—*because we did not seek Him in the way He ordained.* (1 Chronicles 15:11-13)

As mentioned, the Ark of the Covenant represented the Glory and the Presence of God. During the time that Eli was the Chief Priest, he was allowing his sons to disgrace the temple (which represented the church). Because of the evil that was taking place, God allowed the children of Israel to suffer a great defeat. Many of the soldiers died in battle. The Ark of the Covenant was stolen from them. Although we know that the true Church consists of the people of God, spiritual leaders must always be careful to teach about respecting the house of God as well. When we are not being obedient to the commandments of God and we are disrespecting His temple (be it the church or our bodies), we are inviting tragedy into our lives. The enemy is "Stealing" the Glory and the Presence of God from us.

> The thief cometh not, but for to steal, and to kill, and to destroy: I am come that they might have life, and that they might have it more abundantly. (John 10:10, KJV)

David rose up and came against the Philistines to retrieve the Ark of the Covenant from their enemies. There is going to come a time when we have to say, "Enough is enough! I want my joy back. I want my peace back. I want my praise back. I want the presence of the Lord back in my life!" The Children of Israel were victorious in battle, and our opening scripture is where they are preparing to bring the Ark of the Covenant back home. Let's look at what they did as the prepared for the Presence and the Glory of the Lord.

> And David called for Zadok and Abiathar the priests, and for the Levites, for Uriel, Asaiah, and Joel, Shemaiah, and Eliel, and Amminadab. (1 Chronicles 15: 11)

Leaders Were Appointed. The Levites were chosen to usher in the presence of the Lord. The purpose of the Worship team is not for entertainment. They have been appointed, anointed, trained and equipped to usher the people of God into the presence of God.

> And said to them, You are the heads of the fathers' houses of the Levites; sanctify yourselves, both you and your brethren, that you may bring up the ark of the Lord, the God of Israel, to the place that I have prepared for it. [13]For because you bore it not [as God directed] at the first, the Lord our God broke forth upon us—*because we did not seek Him in the way He ordained.* (1 Chronicles 15:12)

They were commanded to sanctify themselves (set apart/holiness). Those who are chosen to lead worship must be living sanctified lives. We understand that no one is perfect and lives totally sin free. The True Worshipper cannot be openly practicing sin, then go into the house of the Lord to lead people into the presence of God. This is why the Presence of God was taken from the Children of Israel. Eli and his sons died in the midst of all of this.

The Place (house/tent) was already prepared (ready) to receive the Presence of the Lord. God prepared local churches throughout the world where the people of God come together to enjoy the Corporate Worship Experience. The care and maintenance of the house was done (administrative duties completed). David (who represented their spiritual covering) ensured that the house was in order prior to bringing the Ark into the tabernacle.

> So David, the elders of Israel, and the captains over thousands went to bring up the ark of the covenant of the Lord out of the house of Obed-edom with joy. [26]And when God helped the Levites who carried the ark of the covenant of the Lord [with a safe start], they offered seven bulls and seven rams. (1 Chronicles 15: 25-26)

David – Represented their Spiritual Covering (i.e. Pastoral Overseer). The Senior Pastor is ultimately responsible for everything that takes place in the Corporate Worship Service. He is the one who will have to answer to God concerning the church. It is very important that the Senior Pastor be a True Worshipper. When this is evident, the congregation will follow their lead.

Elders and **Captains** – Represented the Auxiliary

Leaders. They went corporately (together) to bring the Ark of the Covenant. There was a united effort to usher in the Presence of the Lord. It would take everyone's participation to usher in the Presence and Glory of the Lord during the Corporate Worship experience.

Levites (Worship Leaders) – When they recognized that it was God who helped them, they offered sacrifices. The number 7 represents completion: "...they *offered seven bulls and seven rams...*" They totally offered the sacrifice of praise unto the Lord. We should give God our all when we praise Him. We should give him the best part of us!

> By him therefore let us offer the sacrifice of praise to God continually, that is, the fruit of our lips giving thanks to his name. (Hebrews 13:15, KJV)

The "Fruit of Our Lips" indicate that there is a verbal declaration on our part. The Worship Leaders assist the congregation to get into the presence of God. They are a very important part of the Corporate Worship Experience.

> And it came to pass, as the ark of the covenant of the LORD came to the city of David, that Michal, the daughter of Saul looking out at a window saw king David dancing and playing: and she despised him in her heart. (1 Chronicles 15:29, KJV)

As David and the rest of the Children of Israel were worshipping God, there were some who were despising them. There were some who didn't participate or get involved with the corporate worship experience. They were spectators and what many in today's generation would call "haters." There are always going to be some people who won't understand our praise and our worship. Some will despise us because of how we praise and worship. This shouldn't stop us from giving God the glory and honor that he deserves. Let's continue to magnify the Lord in our corporate worship experience. Note the below progression of how our corporate worship can lead to individual blessings.

- Individual worship leads to corporate worship
- Corporate worship leads to a corporate anointing
- Corporate anointing leads to corporate blessings
- Corporate blessings flows in to the individual worshipper.

3

The Character of a True Worshipper

You may be asking, "What does character and worship have in common?" Before I attempt to answer that question, let me give you a few thoughts to ponder on. If there were one book of the Bible that comes to mind when you think about wisdom, it would probably be Proverbs. Solomon was one of the wisest men to every walk the earth and he gave us many principles of wisdom in his book. If you were to think of end-time prophecy, the book of Revelation is where you would probably start. The book of Genesis is usually referred to as the book of beginnings. Now, what book of the Bible would you normally think about when you think about praise and worship? The majority of us would probably think about the book of Psalms. Let's look at how God decided to begin the book of Psalms (songs, praise and worship).

> Blessed is the man that walketh not in the counsel of the ungodly, nor standeth in the way of sinners, nor sitteth in the seat of the scornful. ²But his delight is in the law of the LORD; and in

his law doth he meditate day and night.
(Psalm 1:1-2, KJV)

As a True Worshipper, our character should be one that demonstrates integrity, trustworthiness, faithfulness and dedication. There are too many church goers who are not totally committed to the things of God. If there are serious deficiencies in our character, this could become a stumbling block for other people. As we review the above scripture, notice that the first chapter of the book of praises is not talking about praise at all. I would think, from a literal standpoint, that God would begin the book of praises talking about praise. Psalm 150 could have been a good place to start. It reads,

> Praise ye the LORD. Praise God in his sanctuary: praise him in the firmament of his power. ²Praise him for his mighty acts: praise him according to his excellent greatness. ³Praise him with the sound of the trumpet: praise him with the psaltery and harp. ⁴Praise him with the timbrel and dance: praise him with stringed instruments and organs. ⁵Praise him upon the loud cymbals: praise him upon the high sounding cymbals. ⁶Let every thing that hath breath praise the LORD. Praise ye the LORD. (Psalm 150:1-6)

Instead, God began the book of praises speaking to us about character. I believe that He is instructing the True Worshippers to beware of people who are unwise and ungodly. He knew that if allowed, the ungodly will infiltrate the minds and hearts of the true worshippers and eventually cause their praises to be perverted.

If we take a closer look at Psalm 1:1, we can see a progression. (*Blessed is the man that walketh not in the counsel of the ungodly...*) First, we see a blessed man walking. He was excited about the things of God and not concerned about selfish motives or desires. He was committed to living a life of worship unto the Lord. His walk was upright and it flowed into his worship experience. He is indeed blessed. At some point during his walk, a subtle transition begian to take place. (...nor standeth in the way of sinners...) This blessed man began to listen to the counsel of the ungodly. Someone began to counsel him and questioned his faith. They may be saying things like, "It doesn't take all of that. You don't have to praise God like that to be saved. You look foolish." This type of negative influence must have had an effect on him because he was no longer walking. Now he stands the way sinners stand (doing what they do). The end state of this man is that he ended up sitting down and being a scorner. (...nor sitteth in the seat of the scornful...) He is now the man who is giving the ungodly counsel to someone else. The cycle will continue as long as those who are blessed heed the counsel of those who are ungodly. God knew the negative impact of this cycle, so he began by giving us a warning. We will review this principle more in the next chapter.

I believe that having a godly character is one of the most important attributes of our walk as True Worshippers. Integrity should be a character trait that identifies who we are. My practical definition of integrity is doing the right thing, for the right reasons whether someone is watching or not. Let's take a more detailed look at this first chapter in the book of Psalms.

> Blessed *is* the man that walketh not in the counsel of the ungodly, nor standeth in the way of sinners, nor sitteth in the seat of the scornful. ²But his delight *is* in the law of the LORD; and in his law doth he meditate day and night. ³And he shall be like a tree planted by the rivers of water, that bringeth forth his fruit in his season; his leaf also shall not wither; and whatsoever he doeth shall prosper. (Psalm 1:1-3, KJV)

I think that it is a safe assumption that most people want to be blessed. However, we must realize that being blessed doesn't necessarily come automatically. Every person in this world must come to the understanding that everything that we do has consequences (whether good or bad). There is a spiritual law that was instituted in the book of Genesis called "Seedtime and Harvest" that is still in effect today. (Genesis 8:22: *While the earth remaineth, seedtime and harvest, and cold and heat, and summer and winter, and day and night shall not cease.*) At an appointed time we all will have to give an account of how we have lived our lives. The question of the hour is "How are you living?" What kinds of seeds are you sowing/planting? What type of fruit are you producing? Will God be pleased with your harvest? If you were accused of being a Christian (a blessed man/woman), would there be enough evidence against you for a conviction?

As True Worshippers, we must always be aware that people are watching us; whether in church or not. As believers, we must set the example for others to emulate. The Apostle Paul encouraged others to follow him as he followed Christ. We have a tremendous opportunity to impact people's lives through the gifts and talents that God has given us. Because we submit our gifts back to God, He can use them for His glory. Let's take a closer look at Psalm 1:1.

> Blessed *is* the man that walketh not in the counsel of the ungodly, nor standeth in the way of sinners, nor sitteth in the seat of the scornful. ²But his delight *is* in the law of the LORD; and in his law doth he meditate day and night. ³And he shall be like a tree planted by the rivers of water, that bringeth forth his fruit in his season; his leaf also shall not wither; and whatsoever he doeth shall prosper. (Psalm 1:1-3, KJV)

Being blessed goes far beyond possessions,

finances and social status. The dictionary defines it as: enjoying happiness or bliss; favored with blessings; happy; highly favored; consecrated; sacred; holy; sanctified: worthy of adoration, reverence, or worship; divinely or supremely favored; fortunate. God began the book of praises (Psalms) talking about being consecrated, holy and sanctified. He wanted us to understand that our praise and our worship are only an outward expression of who we really are. As we worship the Lord, what's in us will come out of us. That's why it is so important for us to monitor what we allow into our spirits. The seeds that are sown into our hearts through our ears and eyes can have an effect on the ministry that we are providing.

> Blessed *is* the man that walketh not in the counsel of the ungodly… (Psalm 1:1-3, KJV)

A blessed man/woman is walking in the divine favor of God. He/She is walking by faith and not by the things that appear. They only listen and adhere to Godly counsel. They are careful of what goes into their spirit. When we are walking in ungodly counsel, the Bible is saying that we are not blessed. We have to know that God is speaking to us through His Word. The word is being sown into the atmosphere and God's word shall not return back void.

> So shall My word be that goes forth out of My mouth: it shall not return to Me void [*without producing any ef-*

> *fect, useless*], but it shall accomplish that which I please and purpose, and it shall prosper in the thing for which I sent it. (Isaiah 55:11, AMP)

Ungodly counsel is any advice that is contrary to the Word of God. What is not of God is of the devil.

> Do not be so deceived and misled! Evil companionships (communion, associations) corrupt and deprave good manners and morals and character. (1 Corinthians 15:33, AMP)

When we receive ungodly counsel, we are allowing the enemy to sow unhealthy seeds into our lives, which will produce an unhealthy harvest.

As True Worshippers, it is very important that we monitor what we allow into our spirits. I personally believe that there are some music that we as believers should not listen to—especially those that are called to minister to others. Any music that does not edify, does not speak life, or that does not promote righteous living should not be in our music library. There are certain types of songs that are specifically designed to create certain moods, attitudes or responses. The enemy has a very big influence in music. If he can sow seeds of unrighteousness through music, then he is being effective at providing ungodly counsel. Let's review a passage of scripture that deals with the power and importance of healthy seeds.

> Another parable put he forth unto them, saying, The kingdom of heaven is likened unto a man which sowed good seed in his field: ²⁵But while men slept, his enemy came and sowed tares among the wheat, and went his way. ²⁶But when the blade was sprung up, and brought forth fruit, then appeared the tares also. ²⁷So the servants of the householder came and said unto him, Sir, didst not thou sow good seed in thy field? from whence then hath it tares? ²⁸He said unto them, An enemy hath done this. The servants said unto him, Wilt thou then that we go and gather them up? ²⁹But he said, Nay; lest while ye gather up the tares, ye root up also the wheat with them. ³⁰Let both grow together until the harvest: and in the time of harvest I will say to the reapers, Gather ye together first the tares, and bind them in bundles to burn them: but gather the wheat into my barn. (Matthew 13:24-30, KJV)

This passage of scriptures is one of a series of parables that Jesus was teaching to the multitude. He would often present principles (sow seeds) to the multitude, and then give revelation of those principles to his disciples (inner circle). In his explanation of the parable in Matthew 13:36-43, this is how Jesus defined the characters:

- **One Who Sows Good Seeds**: Jesus
- **Field**: The World
- **Good Seeds**: Children of the Kingdom
- **Tares**: Children of the Wicked One
- **One who sows tares**: The enemy (the devil)
- **Harvest**: End of the World
- **Reapers**: The angels

Jesus approached this passage of scripture from a universal perspective. He was letting the Disciples know that the enemy's desire is to infiltrate and disrupt the Kingdom of God. However, let's view this from a more personal perspective. Who are you allowing to sow into your life? This includes the music that we listen to and the television shows that we watch. We must understand that there are many voices speaking to us at any given time. Which of these voices are getting most of our attention? Let me submit to you that the voice that you hear more frequently will more than likely be the voice that you yield to the most. The enemy is waiting to find us sleeping so he can sow "tares" into our lives (counsel of the ungodly). Let's look at some definitions relating to this scripture:

Sleeping: inactive, resting, hidden, undeveloped. A tare is actually "false grain." It looks like wheat in its early stages, but when it is fully developed the true nature is revealed. There are some things that the enemy will sow into your life that appears to be wheat, but when it is fully developed you will see that it was only a tare that has no value.

> Who changed the truth of God into a lie, and worshipped and served the creature more than the Creator, who is blessed for ever. Amen. (Romans 1:25, KJV)

If we are not careful, we can waste time and energy nurturing, pruning, working, watering, clipping, etc. something that is designed for our destruction.

> …nor standeth in the way of sinners…
> (Psalm 1:1, KJV)

A blessed man/woman is not standing submissive and inactive where sinners walk. They are mindful of their surroundings and the things that are spoken into their spirits. They understand the power of words and that life and death are in the power of the tongue.

> Death and life *are* in the power of the tongue: and they that love it shall eat the fruit thereof. (Proverbs 18:21, KJV)

If we love life, then we will speak life and surround ourselves with people who speak life. If we love death, then we will speak death and surround ourselves with people who do the same. Notice that this "blessed" man started out <u>walking</u> until he listened to the counsel of the ungodly (receiving bad seed/ungodly counsel). Now we see him standing in a place of idleness and inactivity.

God's Word is Good Seed! The enemy will always try to contradict what God says. Sometimes the enemy will even try to use the Word against us by misquoting or taking it out of context. This is why the Bible tells us to study the word of God and meditate on it. We must be sure that every word that we receive is from the Lord and does not conflict with scripture.

> The thief cometh not, but for to steal, and to kill, and to destroy: I am come that they might have life, and that they might have *it* more abundantly. (John 10:10, KJV)

Jesus comes to sow life (the opposite of what the devil wants to do). Take a look at the below illustration:

DEVIL – drop the "**D**" and you have **EVIL**

Everything that the devil sows is evil. He is the father of lies. He may even tell you something that is true, but it will not be the Truth (the Word). For example, he may say that you are sick (which may be true), but the Truth is that you are healed by the stripes of Jesus.

EVIL is **LIVE** spelled backwards.

If the thief comes to steal, give your life to Jesus and get the reverse: God will replenish; If he comes to kill, Jesus will give you life; If he comes to destroy, Jesus comes to rebuild.

> ...nor sitteth in the seat of the

> scornful... (Psalm 1:1, KJV)

A blessed man/woman is not sitting in the assembly of the unrighteous. They understand that they are the light of the world and that darkness cannot comprehend (overtake) them. They are on a mission to advance the Kingdom of God by sowing seeds of the word every time they have an opportunity. They create an atmosphere for God to move and expect Him to provide an opportunity for them to minister the Word to a lost soul.

> But his delight *is* in the law of the LORD; and in his law doth he meditate day and night. (Psalm 1:2)

A blessed man/woman meditates on God's Word day and night. To meditate means to examine, to experience, to contemplate, to give thought to, and to evaluate. To maintain our blessed status, we must learn and apply principles of the Word of God to our lives. Meditation on God's Word will give us a greater revelation and appreciation of Who He is. This will cause us to develop a closer relationship with Him.

> Study to shew thyself approved unto God, a workman that needeth not to be ashamed, rightly dividing the word of truth. (2 Timothy 2:15, KJV)

When we do this, we are sowing Good Seed into our lives which will produce Good Fruit.

> Be not deceived; God is not mocked:

> for whatsoever a man soweth, that shall he also reap. ⁸For he that soweth to his flesh shall of the flesh reap corruption; but he that soweth to the Spirit shall of the Spirit reap life everlasting. ⁹And let us not be weary in well doing: for in due season we shall reap, if we faint not. (Galatians 6:7-9 KJV)

Always remember that *God determines when our "due season" is.*

> And he shall be like a tree planted by the rivers of water, that bringeth forth his fruit in his season; his leaf also shall not wither; and whatsoever he doeth shall prosper. (Psalm 1:3)

If we truly confess to be blessed then our fruit should reveal that we are blessed. Being blessed goes far beyond possessions, finances and social status. There are characteristics of a blessed man/woman that reveal who we really are and who we belong to. Let us continue to receive the Good Seed that God is sowing, nurture that seed and produce a healthy harvest for the Kingdom!

> Either make the tree good, and his fruit good; or else make the tree corrupt, and his fruit corrupt: for the tree is known by *his* fruit. (Matthew 12:33, KJV)

A True Worshipper has a heart for God and for the people of God. Their desire should be to deposit good seeds into those that they serve. If we have the Word of God in us and feed ourselves with good seeds, then we are going to have a positive influence and deposit positive seeds in others. We have a responsibility to teach and train the next generation of worshipers, dancers, singers and musicians. We must not only teach them with our words, but we must teach them with our lives. Our lights should shine so that our Father will be glorified.

4

The Fall of Lucifer

As True Worshippers, we must understand that we have a significant responsibility. We assist in setting the atmosphere for a divine visitation. We help create an environment where people will begin to be drawn to the Spirit of God and ultimately give their lives to Christ. We must ensure that our spirits remain open and receptive to what God is going to speak during the worship service. Why do we even care? We care, because a True Worshipper is not just a church attendee. We are concerned about the spiritual atmosphere of our worship service. We are concerned about the souls that God is going to bring into our presence. We want to remove any distractions from them receiving all that God has for them. The enemy doesn't want us to truly worship God because he wants those distractions to be there. He wants people to make excuses as to why there is no change in their lives. He doesn't want people to enter into worship. Our adversary is truly an enemy of the cross. How did this come to be? Well let's look into the Word of God.

> Moreover the word of the LORD came unto me, saying, [12]Son of man, take up

a lamentation upon the king of Tyrus, and say unto him, Thus saith the Lord GOD; Thou sealest up the sum, full of wisdom, and perfect in beauty. [13]Thou hast been in Eden the garden of God; every precious stone was thy covering, the sardius, topaz, and the diamond, the beryl, the onyx, and the jasper, the sapphire, the emerald, and the carbuncle, and gold: the workmanship of thy tabrets and of thy pipes was prepared in thee in the day that thou wast created. [14]Thou art the anointed cherub that covereth; and I have set thee so: thou wast upon the holy mountain of God; thou hast walked up and down in the midst of the stones of fire. [15]Thou wast perfect in thy ways from the day that thou wast created, till iniquity was found in thee. [16]By the multitude of thy merchandise they have filled the midst of thee with violence, and thou hast sinned: therefore I will cast thee as profane out of the mountain of God: and I will destroy thee, O covering cherub, from the midst of the stones of fire. [17]Thine heart was lifted up because of thy beauty, thou hast corrupted thy wisdom by reason of thy brightness: I will cast thee to the ground, I will lay thee before kings, that they may behold thee. (Ezek 28:11-17)

This passage of scripture is describing the fall of Lucifer. Before Satan became the fallen devil that he is, his name was Lucifer and he was one of the chief angels in heaven. He was the most beautiful of God's angels and was responsible for creating the atmosphere for worship in heaven. Note some of the characteristics of Lucifer: He was full of wisdom and perfect in beauty. His body was covered with precious stones. There were tabrets built within him. The word tabret in the Hebrew is *Toph; which meant* tambourine. This represented percussion instruments. He also had pipes built within (which represented wind instruments i.e. flutes, trumpets, etc.) The Bible calls him the anointed angel (Cherub) that covered the atmosphere with worship (music). He was one of the chief angels in heaven so this means that he was in an elevated position. Let's look at another scripture that makes reference to Lucifer.

> How art thou fallen from heaven, O Lucifer, son of the morning! how art thou cut down to the ground, which didst weaken the nations! [13]For thou hast said in thine heart, I will ascend into heaven, I will exalt my throne above the stars of God: I will sit also upon the mount of the congregation, in the sides of the north: [14]I will ascend above the heights of the clouds; I will be like the most High. [15]Yet thou shalt be brought down to hell, to the sides of the pit. [16]They that see thee shall

> narrowly look upon thee, and consider thee, saying, Is this the man that made the earth to tremble, that did shake kingdoms; (Isaiah 14:12-16)

This passage of scripture speaks of the character of Lucifer and the true cause of his fall. As I mentioned earlier, Lucifer was in an elevated position and was in charge of leading the host of heaven in worship. At some point in his ministry, his motives began to change. No longer did he want to worship God, but he wanted the angels to worship him. Because of his tainted character, he no longer wanted to be the leader of worship unto God. He wanted to be like God. This may seem like a harmless gesture to the average person but we must look at the spiritual significance of what was happening. There is a difference in wanting to be a reflection of who God is and wanting God's position and power. This is where Lucifer made his mistake. He wanted God's position.

Many True Worshippers, singers and musicians fall into the same trap that Lucifer did. They start out with pure motives and intents, but publicity and notoriety sometimes has a negative effect. Jesus made reference to the fall of Lucifer in his teachings.

> And he said unto them, I beheld Satan as lightning fall from heaven. (Luke 10:18)

Because of Lucifer's sin, he was cast down out of

heaven. He didn't fall by himself, but there were 1/3 of the angels that fell with him. These are they that heeded his "ungodly counsel" and decided to rebel against God.

> For if God spared not the angels that sinned, but cast *them* down to hell, and delivered *them* into chains of darkness, to be reserved unto judgment; (2 Peter 2:4)

When Satan was cast out of heaven, he was stripped of his power and authority. His name was changed which was representative of a demotion. Even with all of that, he didn't loose his ability to influence. Remember, he convinced 1/3 of the angels to rebel with him.

> And prevailed not; neither was their place found any more in heaven. 9 And the great dragon was cast out, that old serpent, called the Devil, and Satan, which deceiveth the whole world: he was cast out into the earth, and his angels were cast out with him. (Revelation 12:8)

Notice some things about Satan before his fall. He was full of wisdom and perfect in beauty (He was smart and knew his craft; flawless in his appearance). He was covered with precious stones (He was a sight to be seen; a shining star). He had tabrets (Heb. Toph Tambourine; represented percussion instruments) and pipes built within (represented wind instruments i.e. flutes, trumpets, etc). Isaiah 14 notes: Noise of thy viols speaks of six stringed instruments i.e. harps, guitars, pianos, etc. He was the "anointed angel that covered" which implied that he was a coverer; a protector, watchman; chief angel. He was in an elevated position and had oversight of the worship in heaven. He was a True Worshipper when he was created.

Now, let's look at the details of his fall. This all started in his heart, then manifested into actions.

I will ascend into heaven: He wanted to exalt himself. The Bible warns about thinking more highly of ourselves than we ought to think. It is one thing to know that God is using us, but we should never lose sight of the fact that we are just conduits for the anointing to flow through.

Above the stars of God: Although he was appointed as the leader, he overstepped his boundaries. He stepped out of his realm of anointing and wanted to be the focus of attention.

Sit Upon the Mount of the congregation: He wanted to be in the high place where everyone could see him. He perfected his gift, but his character was out of order.

I will be like the Most High: This is a deceptive character trait. He was saying that he wanted to be like God not in the sense of imitation. He was looking at it from a power perspective. He wanted to control the universe and the affairs of heaven.

> Thou wast perfect in thy ways from the day that thou wast created, till iniquity was found in thee. [16] By the multitude of thy merchandise they have filled the midst of thee with violence, and thou hast sinned: therefore I will cast thee as profane out of the mountain of God: and I will destroy thee, O covering cherub, from the midst of the stones of fire. [17] Thine heart was lifted up because of thy beauty, thou hast corrupted thy wisdom by reason of thy brightness: I will cast thee to the ground, I will lay thee before kings, that they may behold thee. (Ezek 28:15-17)

Iniquity was found in him. The definition of Iniquity is "a violation of right or duty." He overstepped his boundaries. He was in violation of his God given assignment. Because of his abundance of gifting and talent, his motives changed. He became Proud and arrogant. He sinned: Sin means to "miss the mark." He was no longer in alignment with God's purpose for creating him. His wisdom was corrupted. His thought pattern and judgment was corrupted because of his spender. Because of his beauty, his heart became lifted up in pride.

The enemy's goal is to try to get us to make the same mistakes that he did. Note the following: There are some areas in our lives that he could use to try to make us fall from grace. Some of us have gained some wisdom and are duty experts in our fields (spiritually/secularly). We are smart and have mastered our craft. We are intelligent, educated, and have ability and influence others. We look good, dress well, smell good, feel good, and we are confident in who we are. We are anointed and we are talented. We can sing, dance, play, pray, prophesy, greet, teach, preach, give, etc. Some of us have positions of authority in the ministry and on our jobs.

There is nothing wrong with us having things or being confident in who we are in Christ. However, we must always remember that there is a battle going on for our souls. The enemy knows that we were created in the image of God, but he wants us to operate like he did. He wants us to become filled with Iniquity (violation of right or duty). He wants us to overstep our boundaries. He wants us to blow our God given assignments. God has established structure and order in the church. This doesn't mean that any position is more important than another; but there are specific functions for areas of ministry. If everyone's goal is to be the greatest servant, we will never overstep our boundaries.

> Likewise, ye younger, submit yourselves unto the elder. Yea, all of you be subject one to another, and be clothed with humility: for God resisteth the proud, and giveth grace to the humble. (1 Peter 5:5)

The enemy doesn't care if we have an abundance of gifts and talents as long as our motives are selfish. His goal is to get us to become proud and arrogant. He wants us to sin. Sin means to "miss the mark". He wants us to be out of alignment with God's purpose for creating us.

> Pride goeth before destruction, and an haughty spirit before a fall. (Proverbs 16:18)

He doesn't want us to know the Word of God, but depend on our own wisdom. This will cause our thought pattern and judgment to be corrupted. We should always be mindful because he will use people to feed into our egos and tell us how beautiful and anointed we are in effort to corrupt our spirits. He wants us to become lifted up in pride.

The word of God is our biggest defense against the enemy. It is the Word of God that is going to cause the transformation of our minds. The Word of God says:

> And be not conformed to this world: but be ye transformed by the renewing of your mind, that ye may prove what is that good, and acceptable, and perfect, will of God. (Romans 12:2)

The transformation from Lucifer to Satan all began from the inner thoughts within his heart. It all started in his heart then manifested physically and spiritually.

5

The Battle for Your Worship

> But the hour cometh, and now is, when the true worshippers shall worship the Father in spirit and in truth: for the Father seeketh such to worship him. (John 4:23)

The battle is really about Worship! Did you know that God is seeking true worshipers and so is Satan? Remember, Satan wanted to be like God. He even tried to trick man into thinking we could be like God (in the wrong perspective).

> For God doth know that in the day ye eat thereof, then your eyes shall be opened, and ye shall be as gods, knowing good and evil. (Genesis 3:5)

That was also the bottom line when the devil tempted Jesus in the wilderness.

> And saith unto him, All these things will I give thee, if thou wilt fall down and worship me. [10]Then saith Jesus unto him, Get thee hence, Satan: for it

> is written, Thou shalt worship the Lord thy God, and him only shalt thou serve. [11]Then the devil leaveth him, and, behold, angels came and ministered unto him. (Matthew 4:9-11)

Before Jesus did any miracles, before His name was great among men, God had to send Him to the wilderness so that His true character could be tested. God had just declared that He was pleased with Jesus, but now Jesus had to prove that He was, in fact, willing to fulfill His call (he had to walk it out himself). Some of us are anointed and have had some prophecies spoken over us, but our character must be intact. The battle with the enemy is his attempt to pervert our praise/worship/music. The devil tries to counter everything that God does to draw followers. Everything that the enemy does is an effort to take the glory from God and have it for himself. He uses God's greatest creation to try to get back at God "See God, you died for these people and they still don't praise you. They'd rather praise me." – Accuser of the brethren.

As True Worshippers, singers and musicians, we must understand that there is a battle that is taking place for our gifts. There will be times that we will be tested and tempted. These are seasons of our lives that are designed to bring out the best in us. We must understand that regardless of what stage we are in our Christian walk, there will be seasons that we must go through. Jesus also went through seasons as He progressed to be the perfect example for us. Although He was without sin, he had to learn some things along the way.

> Though he were a Son, yet learned he obedience by the things which he suffered; (Hebrews 5:8)

Lets take a look at three seasons that Jesus experienced. We will extract some points and principals (Kingdom Keys) that Jesus teaches us by His example. We will talk about the following seasons that we all must go through: A Season of Preparation, A Season of Testing and A Season of Service (Ministry).

> His parents went to Jerusalem every year at the Feast of the Passover. [42]And when He was twelve years old, they went up to Jerusalem according to the custom of the feast. [43]When they had finished the days, as they returned, the Boy Jesus lingered behind in Jerusalem. And Joseph and His mother[a] did not know it; [44]but supposing Him to have been in the company, they went a day's journey, and sought Him among their relatives and acquaintances. [45]So when they did not find Him, they returned to Jerusalem, seeking Him. [46]Now so it was that after three days they found Him in the temple, sitting in the midst of the teachers, both listening to them and asking them questions. [47]And all who heard Him were astonished at His

> understanding and answers. [48] So when they saw Him, they were amazed; and His mother said to Him, "Son, why have You done this to us? Look, Your father and I have sought You anxiously." [49]And He said to them, "Why did you seek Me? Did you not know that I must be about My Father's business?" [50]But they did not understand the statement which He spoke to them. Jesus Advances in Wisdom and Favor [51]Then He went down with them and came to Nazareth, and was subject to them, but His mother kept all these things in her heart. (Luke 2:41-51)

Season 1: A Season of Preparation

As we look at the early life of Jesus we will notice that not much is spoken about his "Preparation" stages. The Gospels are detailed in explaining the circumstances surrounding his birth, but then it appears as if Jesus disappears.

> And the child grew and became strong in spirit; and he lived in the desert until he appeared publicly to Israel. (Luke 1:80, NIV)

Jesus Grew (increased; became greater) and became strong in spirit: He spent time in the desert preparing before he made any public appearances.

We must all go through the **PROCESS** of growing. Jesus "BECAME" strong in spirit. Many people want to be overnight sensations or instant millionaires (lottery, shortcuts, reality shows, gimmicks, media attention, etc.). There are some things that God needs to do in us as He prepares us for Kingdom work. Everyone that God used in scripture went through a development process (Abraham, Moses, Elijah, Samuel, David, Peter, Paul, etc.) The next time that we see Jesus, he is 12 years old teaching in the temple.

> And it came to pass, that after three days ***they found him*** in the temple, sitting in the midst of the doctors, both hearing them, and asking them questions. [47]And all that heard him were astonished at his understanding and answers. (Luke 2:46-47)

Joseph and Mary went yearly to Jerusalem for the feast of the Passover. Jesus was twelve years old, which was significant in the Jewish culture. Under Jewish Law, children are not obligated to observe the commandments. At the age of 13 (12 for girls), children become obligated to observe the commandments. This shows that Jesus was ahead of His peers. Not only did he observe the commandments, but he understood them well enough to have intelligent conversation with teachers of the Law. After the festivities, Joseph and Mary began their journey back home and didn't realize that Jesus wasn't with them, so they turned around (repented) to find Jesus – Selah! Ironically, when they found him, he was in the same place that they left him (in the temple courtyard).

Many people are carrying on with their lives and don't even realize that they left Jesus behind. We can get so busy being who we are that we schedule Jesus out of our schedules. Remember that all aspects of our lives as Kingdom Citizens should be subject to the King. We must seek him for spiritual guidance, vocational guidance, social guidance, financial guidance, educational guidance, physical guidance, etc. We must acknowledge the fact that we left Jesus behind (He didn't leave us). We simply need to REPENT (turn from our sins and toward God). Jesus had been in the temple developing relationships/planting seeds.

Listening: Jesus did this to connect with the people. Even at 12 years old, Jesus was listening and asking questions. Before ministering to needy people or telling them about the kingdom, He took the time to listen. He knew that to connect with people's hearts, He had to use his ears. All that heard him were amazed at his understanding and his answers.

> And Jesus increased in wisdom and stature, and in favour with God and man. (Luke 2:52)

Our horizontal relationships with people are closely tied to our vertical relationship with God. The Bible says that Jesus increased in wisdom, in stature and in favor with God and Man. As Christians, it is important for us to develop a relationship with God. We must also develop relationships with those that we will have to minister to.

We cannot be so heavenly minded that we are no earthly good. Not only are we supposed to develop and operate in the Gifts of the Spirit, but there also must be evidence of the Fruit of the Spirit in our lives.

> But the fruit of the Spirit is love, joy, peace, longsuffering, gentleness, goodness, faith, [23]Meekness, temperance: against such there is no law. (Galatians 5: 22-23)

As Jesus moved closer to beginning His public ministry; there was another season that He had to go through. Most people don't realize it, but Jesus spent 30 years preparing in private for a 3½-year public ministry. The next season the Jesus went through was a *season of testing*.

Season 2: A Season of Testing

Jesus showed up at the Jordan River and was baptized by John the Baptist. This was evidence to God and to the world that Jesus was committed to the purpose of God for his life. Baptism is an outward expression of an inward change. It was after this step of faith; act of obedience; stepping out of the box – that the Season of Testing began. The Spirit of God descended upon Him (Empowerment). God the Father validated Him.

> And lo a voice from heaven, saying, This is my beloved Son, in whom I am well pleased. (Matthew 3:17)

The Spirit of God led him into the wilderness to be tempted of the devil. There is a big difference between temptation and testing. God will allow us to be tested to build us up. The enemy tempts us with the intent of destroying us.

> Let no man say when he is tempted, I am tempted of God: for God cannot be tempted with evil, neither tempteth he any man: [14]But every man is tempted, when he is drawn away of his own lust, and enticed. [15]Then when lust hath conceived, it bringeth forth sin: and sin, when it is finished, bringeth forth death. (James 1:13-15, KJV)

God will allow the enemy to temp us to work some ungodly things out of us and establish Godly characteristics within us. If He allowed his only begotten Son to be tempted with all types of things, we can expect to have to deal with temptations as well.

> For we do not have a High Priest who cannot sympathize with our weaknesses, but was in all *points* tempted as *we are, yet* without sin. (Hebrews 4:15, NKJV)

And Jesus being full of the Holy Ghost returned from Jordan, and was led by the Spirit into the wilderness, ²Being forty days tempted of the devil. And in those days he did eat nothing: and when they were ended, he afterward hungered. ³And the devil said unto him, If thou be the Son of God, command this stone that it be made bread. ⁴And Jesus answered him, saying, It is written, That man shall not live by bread alone, but by every word of God. ⁵And the devil, taking him up into an high mountain, shewed unto him all the kingdoms of the world in a moment of time. ⁶And the devil said unto him, All this power will I give thee, and the glory of them: for that is delivered unto me; and to whomsoever I will I give it. ⁷If thou therefore wilt worship me, all shall be thine. ⁸And Jesus answered and said unto him, Get thee behind me, Satan: for it is written, Thou shalt worship the Lord thy God, and him only shalt thou serve. ⁹And he brought him to Jerusalem, and set him on a pinnacle of the temple, and said unto him, If thou be the Son of God, cast thyself down from hence: ¹⁰For it is written, He shall give his angels charge over thee, to keep thee: ¹¹And in their hands they shall bear thee up, lest at

> any time thou dash thy foot against a stone. ¹²And Jesus answering said unto him, It is said, Thou shalt not tempt the Lord thy God. ¹³And when the devil had ended all the temptation, he departed from him for a season. ¹⁴And Jesus returned in the power of the Spirit into Galilee: and there went out a fame of him through all the region round about. ¹⁵And he taught in their synagogues, being glorified of all. (Luke 4:1-15)

It is important for us to depend on the Word of God during our season of testing. Jesus faced three major temptations during His 40 day wilderness experience. The enemy approached Him and tried to entice Him through the following temptations:

Practical Needs: He tried to get Jesus to act apart from God in order to meet a practical need. During the season of testing, it will appear as if God has abandoned you in your time of need. It may seem as if He isn't hearing your prayers or responding to your call. The enemy will try to present "possible solutions" that are totally contrary to God's will for your life. We must always respond with the Word of God. If the solution doesn't line up with the Word of God then it should be rejected. Remember that it is a test.

> Knowing this, that the trying of your faith worketh patience. ⁴But let patience have *her* perfect work, that ye

> may be perfect and entire, wanting nothing. (James 1:3-4)

God will always provide for his children.

> But my God shall supply all your need according to his riches in glory by Christ Jesus. (Philippians 4:19)

Spiritual Gifting: He tried to urge Jesus to use His giftedness for self-profit or to draw a crowd. The enemy was trying to get Jesus to operate in self "**PRIDE".** This is the true nature of the enemy and the principle reason that he was kicked out of heaven. Our gifts, talents and abilities should always be used to glorify God.

> Let your light so shine before men, that they may see your good works, and glorify your Father which is in heaven. (Matthew 5:16)

> A man's gift maketh room for him, and bringeth him before great men. (Proverbs 18:16)

Personal Worship: He tried to convince Jesus to get ahead by linking up with a power other than God. During the testing season, be mindful of those things or people that will try to distract you. Be mindful of people in your life that have been planted by the enemy to get you to misuse your gifts, talents and abilities (your anointing). Some people can frustrate your purpose because they are not supposed to be in your life during this season. We must identify those people who are in our lives forever and those who are supposed to be only for a season.

Season 3: A Season of Service (Ministry)

> And Jesus returned in the power of the Spirit into Galilee: and there went out a fame of him through all the region round about. ¹⁵And he taught in their synagogues, being glorified of all. (Luke 4:14-15)

It was only after a Season of Preparation and a Season of Testing that Jesus entered into his Season of Service (Ministry). We must be willing to submit to the process of development if we are going to be effective in what God has called us to do. Notice that Jesus returned "In the Power of the Spirit" to Galilee. When we allow God to work in our lives and submit to the development process, He will empower us to complete the work that he started in us.

> Being confident of this very thing, that he which hath begun a good work in you will perform it until the day of Jesus Christ. (Philippians 1:6)

Regardless of what level of ministry we are at we will go through seasons of Preparation, Testing, and Service. We must understand that God is progressive and expects us to grow. Let's submit to the development process and embrace the season that we are in. God is preparing us to fulfill a Kingdom Assignment. Allow Him to perform a perfect work in you and surrender to His will for your life.

6

Worship is a Weapon

In previous chapters, we have learned that we were created to praise and worship God. God is seeking True Worshippers. John 4:24 says, "*God is a Spirit: and they that worship him must worship him in spirit and in truth.*" This means that we must worship with our "spirits" and in "truth" (in accordance with His Word). We talked about the importance of the corporate worship experience. We learned that we need each other as we strive to become True Worshipers. Now, we want to talk about "Worship is a Weapon." We are going to learn that there are forces that come against us when we make the decision to become a True Worshiper. We are also going to learn the weapons and power we have at our disposal when we praise and worship the Lord. Now we are going to talk a little about Paul and Silas. Our scripture is the end of this particular story, but lets go up a few verses to see how they got to this point.

> And it came to pass, as we went to prayer, a certain damsel possessed with a spirit of divination met us, which brought her masters much gain by soothsaying: [17]The same followed Paul

> and us, and cried, saying, These men are the servants of the most high God, which shew unto us the way of salvation. [18]And this did she many days. But Paul, being grieved, turned and said to the spirit, I command thee in the name of Jesus Christ to come out of her. And he came out the same hour. (Acts 16:16-18)

Paul and Silas were being about the Father's business (advancing the Kingdom of God). There was a woman following them as they went about doing ministry. On the surface, it looked like as if she was a faithful supporter. "…*These men are the servants of the most high God, which shew unto us the way of salvation…*" In all reality, she was being influenced by an evil spirit. When we are being about the Father's business, the enemy will assign evil spirits to distract us. We must evaluate all of our activities and people in our lives to determine if they are our assignment or just a distraction of the enemy. Paul operated in the Anointing and recognized that something was not right. When we are living a life of *worship*, we will be able to recognize those spirits that do not line up. Finally, Paul casts out the evil spirit and this woman became clean. She could no longer make money for her masters.

> And when her masters saw that the hope of their gains was gone, they caught Paul and Silas, and drew them into the marketplace unto the rulers,

> [20]And brought them to the magistrates, saying, These men, being Jews, do exceedingly trouble our city, [21]And teach customs, which are not lawful for us to receive, neither to observe, being Romans. (Acts 16:19-21)

This woman's masters became upset at Paul and Silas and "drew them into the marketplace". To me this means that they were being set up. The enemy was trying to set a trap for them. When we are True Worshipers and truly walking in our callings, the enemy will try to set traps for us. He will try to lure us into conversations and activities to get us off purpose. We must always be mindful of who we are and what our assignment is.

> And the multitude rose up together against them: and the magistrates rent off their clothes, and commanded to beat them. [23]And when they had laid many stripes upon them, they cast them into prison, charging the jailor to keep them safely: [24]Who, having received such a charge, thrust them into the inner prison, and made their feet fast in the stocks. (Acts 16:22-24)

Paul and Silas were lured into town by these "deceivers," then their accusers stirred up the crowd against them. They were stripped, beaten with many stripes, bound with stocks, then thrown in the inner prison (perhaps what we call a dungeon).

Roman stocks were not only made to keep prisoners from escaping, but were made with holes wide enough apart as to stretch the legs and bruise the feet to cause great pain and injury. The enemy likes to lure us into situations that are going to cause us to be stripped, bound, beaten and isolated. He will try to strip us of our purity and dignity by causing us to sin. This affects our ability to truly worship God. He will place situations in our lives that will cause us pain, grief and suffering. This creates a distraction, because we can't focus on worshiping God or ministering to others. He will try to tie up our time and our resources, which creates stress and anxiety. He will attempt to bind us to un-forgiveness, distrust, suspicion, doubt, guilt, anger and bitterness. All of these hinder us from worshiping God in Spirit and in Truth. The enemy loves to separate and isolate believers from their life source.

> And at midnight Paul and Silas prayed, and sang praises unto God: and the prisoners heard them. [26]And suddenly there was a great earthquake, so that the foundations of the prison were shaken: and immediately all the doors were opened, and every one's bands were loosed. (Acts 16:25-26)

Even in the midst of great adversity they found the time and strength to pray and sing praises unto God. When we find ourselves in adverse situations, we must know and understand that there is power in our praise. First we must take **time** to praise and worship God. Next we must gather up the strength to praise and worship God. Emotional strength – when our situation suggests otherwise. Physical strength – when we are tired or sick in our bodies. Spiritual strength – when it seems as if all hope is gone. Paul and Silas made it a point to put Psalm 34 into practical use: "I will bless the Lord at all times, His praise shall continually be in my mouth."

The Bible says that they prayed and praised "at midnight." Midnight: a point between yesterday and tomorrow—in the mean time. Not where I was, but not where I'm going to be either. This can be a place of vulnerability, or a place of advantage. In a defensive posture, we are vulnerable to attacks. In an offensive posture, we are putting the enemy on alert. Paul and Silas put the pressure on the enemy by praising and worshipping God in the midst of their situation. They were in a state of physical discomfort – even though they didn't really feel like praying or praising they knew where they could find peace. They were offering the sacrifice of praise. They weren't praying for God to get them out of their situation, but when praises go up blessing come down.

> And at midnight Paul and Silas prayed, and sang praises unto God: and the prisoners heard them. [26]And suddenly there was a great earthquake, so that the foundations of the prison were shaken: and immediately all the doors

were opened, and every one's bands were loosed. (Acts 16:25-26)

The prisoners heard them, so they must have been making some noise (Shabach). We must make a verbal declaration when we praise God. There was a great earthquake, which means that God moved on their behalf. We can move heaven and earth when we praise. The foundations of the prison were shaken. Our praise can break the chains of the things that have been binding us up. Immediately the doors opened. Our praise can produce instant results. We can receive miracles if we expect them. The Word says that "...everyone's bands were loosed." Sometimes your praise will be the key to someone else's deliverance. Praise God in the midst of adversity. Pray in the midst of trouble. Regardless of what we are going through or what situations arise in our lives, we must praise God in the midst of our troubles. When the forces of evil are against us, we should turn up our level of praise and worship. Remember that your praise and worship can cause the earth to move and heaven to respond.

7

Ministering Through Adversities

I have been in the church for most of my life and have seen and met all types of saints. I've met people that struggle from week to week trying to make ends meet and I've met some that are millionaires. I've met those that have one foot in the church and the other one in the club and those that are truly sold out for Christ. I have been in churches where you can feel the love when you walk in the door and there really is a genuine sense of fellowship among the believers. I've also been in settings where the police had to escort a saint off of the premises. Think it not strange that all of these types of people are in the church. If the truth were told, all of us have some issues that we are working out in our lives. There are some seasons that we abound and others that we are abased. The problem is that most of us are not content in the state that we are in. However, if we are going to be True Worshippers, we must be willing to die to ourselves and be transparent. There are others going through the same thing that we have been through and they don't know how they are going to make it. We have to release our testimonies into the atmosphere so someone else can be released. This is not always easy because we feel safe behind our masks. We don't want folks to get too close, because they might see the real us (and we're not ready for them to see that part of us yet). Let's take a look in scripture at a man that was in the eye of the public but was dealing with some major issues.

> Now Naaman, captain of the host of the king of Syria, was a great man with his master, and honourable, because <u>by him the LORD had given deliverance unto Syria</u>: he was also <u>a mighty man in valour</u>, <u>*but he was* a leper</u>. (II Kings 5:1)

So, who was this man called Naaman? The Bible identified his official title as "Captain of the host" of Syria. This would be equivalent to a senior Commanding General in the military. He was a very powerful man who worked very close to the king. We can assume that he had made his way up through the ranks proving himself to his leaders and winning many battles. He was a proven warrior and had gained the favor of his seniors and subordinates. The Bible even states that he found favor with the king and that he was honorable and mighty in valor. Even with all of this favor and public recognition and service, Naaman was dealing with some serious issues. Naaman was a leper**.** Leprosy is a disabling, deforming disease, slowly progressing throughout the life of the leper but not usually cutting that life short. Management of leprosy involves social, vocational, medical, rehabilitative, orthopedic, and reconstructive surgical services. This is a condition that should have caused him to be a public outcast. More than likely he was in a constant state on physical and emotional pain.

Regardless of how great Naaman was in the sight of the public or in the eyes of the king, he had some problems that ran deeper that most people probably realized. How did he survive in a public position with a major illness? It was custom in those days for people with leprosy to be public outcasts. Maybe he kept his armor on in public where no one could see his condition. Even if the public couldn't see his condition, those closest too him knew what was going on with him because they had to deal with it too. Leprosy is not a highly infectious disease, but prolonged intimate family contact could cause it to spread from one person to another. His family saw the daily pain as he climbed off of his horse in the evenings. They helped change the bandages (**under the armor**) that had stuck to the sores from the blood and sweat. They knew that as long as this problem persisted, there was a greater chance of them catching this disease.

Surely the king must have known of his condition. Maybe he still allowed him to continue to serve because of his skills and what he had to offer. This shows a positive character trait in Naaman. He showed personal discipline with the ability to function under extreme pressure and in difficult circumstances. He knew how to put aside his personal problems to lead soldiers and win battles.

Regardless of all public applause and victory, Naaman was still a leper.

> Finally, my brethren, be strong in the Lord, and in the power of his might. [11] Put on the whole armour of God, that ye may be able to stand against the wiles of the devil. [12] For we wrestle not against flesh[b] and blood, but against principalities, against powers, against the rulers of the darkness of this world, against spiritual wickedness in high *places.* [13] Wherefore take unto you the whole armour of God, that ye may be able to withstand in the evil day, and having done all, to stand. [14] Stand therefore, having your loins girt about with truth, and having on the breastplate of righteousness; [15] And your feet shod with the preparation of the gospel of peace; [16] Above all, taking the shield of faith, wherewith ye shall be able to quench all the fiery darts of the wicked. [17] And take the helmet of salvation, and the sword of the Spirit, which is the word of God: [18] Praying always with all prayer and supplication in the Spirit, and watching thereunto with all perseverance and supplication for all saints; (Ephesians 6:10-18)

There are many True Worshippers, singers, musicians and dancers are just like Naaman. We put our church face on (whole armor of God) and do what we do. We are highly anointed, divinely appointed, too blessed to be stressed and can't be depressed, etc. We have found favor with our leadership and those that we serve (we can pray, sing, preach, teach, cook, type, play, dance, prophesy, etc.). However, we have issues that we don't want anyone to know about because it may change the way that they see us. What is your form of leprosy? What is hiding under your armor that needs to be dealt with? Let me identify a few things that could be going on in our lives that we tend to cover up:

The Past: The inability to get beyond what we once did or what has happened to us can be one of the greatest hindrances to us becoming True Worshippers. Some of us have some things in our past that we are not proud of. We have done some things that have hurt our families, our friends and ourselves. We are being held hostage to these things because we have not asked God to forgive us. In addition, many of us have been hurt, misused, abused, talked about or have been violated in ways that we can't even talk about. Those who we trusted have hurt us. We have been betrayed and taken advantage of. The inability to release the past is a form of leprosy that will slowly destroy us. The Bible gives us clear instructions on how to remedy this problem.

> Brethren, I count not myself to have apprehended: but *this* one thing *I do*, forgetting those things which are be-

hind, and reaching forth unto those things which are before, [14]I press toward the mark for the prize of the high calling of God in Christ Jesus. (Philippians 3:13 -14)

Fleshly Desires: As True Worshippers, we have to be mindful of the activities that we partake in. We must monitor all of our relationships and keep them pure. By doing this, we can reduce the probability that we will fall in to sin. Our flesh must be controlled if we are going to really be the people who God called us to be. As mentioned in previous chapters, the enemy is trying to destroy us and he will use any means necessary. Many times he will use the very thing that we like to destroy us. The devil is not going to come at us in a red suit with a pointy tail and a pitchfork in his hand. He is going to come just the way we like. If you like tall women, he will disguise himself as a tall woman. If you like short men, he will disguise himself as a short man. He is willing to do anything to draw us into his trap to cause our destruction. Our defense against the enemy is the Word of God. To do the will of God is to obey His Word. The more of God's Word that we have in us, the more power we will have to overcome the lusts of the flesh.

> Love not the world, neither the things *that are* in the world. If any man love the world, the love of the Father is not in him. [16] For all that *is* in the world, the lust of the flesh, and the lust of the

> eyes, and the pride of life, is not of the Father, but is of the world. [17] And the world passeth away, and the lust thereof: but he that doeth the will of God abideth for ever. (I John 2:15-17)

Slothfulness: What is slothfulness? It is laziness, loafing, malingering, idleness, sluggish, etc. Many True Worshippers singers, musicians, dancers, producers, and songwriters want to achieve greatness, but they are waiting for it to fall into their laps. They assume that someone is just going to walk up to them and offer them a recording contact. While anything is possible with God, this is not the way it normally happens. Many people don't want to put in the time that it takes to be great, but they want the fame that comes with being great. These people are slothful. How do we recognize that we're being slothful? Let's look at a few scriptures.

> A slothful man hideth his hand in his bosom, and will not so much as bring it to his mouth again. (Proverbs 19:24)

A slothful man will not even want to feed himself (spiritually). They will not study the Word of God for themselves, but they will wait to come to church to be hand fed. They won't apply the word that they have received to their lives.

> Slothfulness casteth into a deep sleep; and an idle soul shall suffer hunger. (Proverbs 19:15)

A slothful man is not excited about the things of God. He is just going through the motions by coming to church just to say that he went or to keep the preacher off of his back (to put a check in the box). He begins to go into a deep sleep wherein things (sin) that should convict him have become somewhat tolerable. This is a state of unconsciousness wherein he is unaware of his spiritual surroundings. His soul begins to be idle (unprofitable). He loses His hunger for Christ. (This is, in fact, losing his desire to live because Jesus is life).

> The way of the slothful man is as an hedge of thorns: but the way of the righteous is made plain. (Proverbs 15:19)

A hedge of thorns is something that is not desirable. It causes pain and discomfort to whatever it touches. The slothful man is a bother to those around him. Jesus had a hedge of thorns placed on His head to add to His sufferings. Paul had a thorn in his side that added to his sufferings. The Bible compares the slothful man to a "hedge of thorns". As True Worshippers, when we are slothful it brings an extra burden upon someone else who has to take up the slack.

> The desire of the slothful killeth him; for his hands refuse to labour. (Proverbs 21: 25)

The slothful man doesn't even want to work. His desire is great, but he is too lazy to work for it. As mentioned, many in the body of Christ want great ministries and want to be used mightily of God, but they don't want to put in the time. They don't want to work. These are people who are usually bitter and frustrated. They are upset with people who are experiencing success in their ministries. They desire greatness, but for some reason are not investing in their gifts. Their desire will kill them. They are slothful.

> The slothful man saith, There is a lion without, I shall be slain in the streets. (Proverbs 22:13)

The slothful person will see danger approaching and won't even put up their defenses. This person takes whatever life dishes out. True Worshippers should always be spiritually discerning and aware of their environment and company. If (and when) we find ourselves in a situation that could compromise our integrity, we should do like Joseph did when Potifer's wife tried to take advantage of him. *Run!* We don't want to be like the slothful man and allow the lion to devour us when we have the power in our hand to do something about it.

These are just a few conditions that could be our leprosy. Others may include rejoicing in iniquity (anxious to exploit another's failures), private disobedience/rebellion (tithes, prayer, study, fasting, etc.), lack of faith (for family members, financial situations, jobs, children, ministry, etc.), and the list goes on.

> So Naaman came with his horses and with his chariot, and stood at the door of the house of Elisha. ¹⁰ And Elisha sent a messenger unto him, saying, Go and wash in Jordan seven times, and thy flesh shall come again to thee, and thou shalt be clean. ¹¹ But Naaman was wroth, and went away, and said, Behold, I thought^c, He will surely come out to me, and stand, and call on the name of the LORD his God, and strike his hand over the place, and recover the leper. (II Kings 5:9-11)

Naaman is presented with the opportunity to be delivered from his disease. He approached the man of God like he "had it going on". Elisha didn't even meet him at the door (a lesson in humility). He was given instructions for his deliverance to take place. Naaman almost missed his blessing because it did not come the way that he thought it should come.

I believe that most of us really want to be healed of our disease and God gives us plenty of opportunities. Some of us can't be delivered because of our armor (i.e. position, reputation, etc.). Many times we don't receive our deliverance because it doesn't come the way we expected. We want the Prophet to specifically call us out and lay hands on us. More often than not, our deliverance will come through simple obedience: lifting your hands, running, shouting, releasing it to God, speaking to your situations, praise and worship, studying the word, church attendance, etc.

> Then went he down, and dipped himself seven times in Jordan, according to the saying of the man of God: and his flesh came again like unto the flesh of a little child, and he was clean. [15]And he returned to the man of God, he and all his company, and came, and stood before him: and he said, Behold, now I know that there is no God in all the earth, but in Israel: now therefore, I pray thee, take a blessing of thy servant. (II Kings 5:14-15)

This is a word for True Worshippers and Praise & Worship Team Leaders. With some encouragement from his servants, Naaman did as he was commanded and received his deliverance. Sometimes, people need extra encouragement to get their breakthrough. Don't be upset at the leaders that are trying to get the believers to "press in". Someone needs that extra push to help them get to the next level. People in today's society are going through all types of situations. The very fact that some made it to church is a miracle. We must be spiritually discerning and know when to stay with a particular song. That song may be what is needed to get the people into position to hear from God. There are many times we will want to go through our song list and sing songs just like the CD. However, we must always be listening to the Holy Spirit and allow us to lead our times of worship.

As we walk about and do the things that God called us to do, let us always remember that we have to be careful that we don't become judgmental. There are issues in all of our lives that we must deal with. Yes we have to function in difficult circumstances and have to overcome adversity, but we still must find a cure for the disease that is killing us from within. Examine ourselves and allow God to do a work in us.

> I acknowledged my sin unto thee, and mine iniquity have I not hid. I said, I will confess my transgressions unto the LORD; and thou forgavest the iniquity of my sin. Selah. (Psalm 32:5)

> If we say that we have no sin, we deceive ourselves, and the truth is not in us. [9] If we confess our sins, he is faithful and just to forgive us *our* sins, and to cleanse us from all unrighteousness. [10] If we say that we have not sinned, we make him a liar, and his word is not in us. (I John 1:8-10)

8

Seasons – Waiting on God

We are living in a very fast paced society. It is more and more important that we position ourselves to be in a place where we can hear from God. One of the greatest strategies of the enemy in our dispensation is to gradually make us so busy that we forget to reserve a place for God in our schedule. If not careful, we can find ourselves busy doing nothing.

I would like to introduce a thought for consideration that may seem to contradict itself. Have you every heard of the term "Hurry Up and Wait?" As a retired Marine, there have been many times when I have been rushed to be someplace, only to find out that I had to wait once I got there. An example of this was when we were preparing to deploy to Iraq. As the senior enlisted person in the company, I had to ensure that my troops were properly trained and ready to fight. There were several times when we rushed to get to a training area only to find out that we had to wait for hours before we could begin our training. During Operation Desert Shield/

Desert Storm, we were given a 48-hour notice to get our gear together because we were going to be shipped out to Saudi Arabia. We did what we needed to do to prepare only to find out that there were no available flights for our unit. We ended up waiting three more days before we left for war. Even though we didn't know exactly when we were leaving, we had to be in the proper position, with the proper equipment, having all of our personal affairs in order to be ready when the call came. Let us take a look into the Word to further explore this idea of "Hurry Up and Wait."

> Wherefore seeing we also are compassed about with so great a cloud of witnesses, let us lay aside every weight, and the sin which so easily beset us, and let us run with patience the race that is set before us. (Hebrews 12:1)

In this race called life, we must be aware of things that can hinder our forward progress. We must be willing to lay aside every weight (heaviness, burden, influence, etc.) that may be a hindrance to our Christian progress. These may not necessarily be sins, but can become a weight if not properly managed. Let's examine some things that can be considered "weight" in our lives that could hinder our forward progress.

The Pursuit of money/happiness/success: There is nothing wrong with having these things as long as they are properly prioritized. If God is not first in our lives, then this is an indication of a life that is "Out of Order". No one wants to invest into something that is out of order. Would you put your money in a soda machine that had a sign on it that said "out of order" on it? Probably not. Then why do we expect God to invest blessings into our lives when we are out of order?

> But seek ye first the kingdom of God, and his righteousness; and all these things shall be added unto you. (Matthew 6:33)

Unfruitful people in our lives; Who are you investing your time into? Are they pulling from you? Some people are in your life for a season and others for a lifetime. Problems come when we try to keep seasonal people in our lives for a lifetime (and vice versa). I would encourage all True Worshippers to be very aware of the people that are in your lives. Many times we want to hang on to people because of various reasons. Maybe they are friends, relatives, have been with you for a long time, have good connections, etc. One thing that we must always remember is that our relationship with God is progressive. We should always be going higher in Him. If the people that you are connected to are not moving in the same direction that God is taking you, you have to let them go. Everyone that you are connected to should be pushing you toward your destiny and not pulling you back into a former life (a familiar place). This doesn't mean that you don't love them or are not concerned about them. This means that you have transitioned to another level in your relationship with God. If they are truly your friends, they will understand that.

I believe there should always be three types of people in our lives: Mentors, Peers, and Mentees. A Mentor is someone who is on a greater level than you are. They should be someone that we admire and trust. A true Mentor is willing to invest their time and talent in us to see us developed and matured in our gifts and callings. They will always challenge us to get better. Our Peers are people who are pretty much on the same level as we are. These are also people who we trust to compliment us when we are doing well and chastise us when we are doing badly. They are not intimidated or jealous of our gifts and talents. Healthy Peer relationships promote growth in both parties. Then there is the Mentee. These are people who are not quite where we are, but we are trying to pull them up to our level. The same responsibilities that we place on our Mentors are passed on to us. This is one way to ensure that the people in our lives are fruitful.

Material Possessions: If the things that you have take more of your time than the things of God, you may want to reevaluate your priorities. As True Worshippers, we are always trying to perfect our gifts. There is always another practice, another rehearsal, another keyboard, another microphone, another soundboard, more choir robes, more banners and streamers, etc. While these things are very important to our ministry, never allow the work of the ministry to take the place of your relationship with God. When this happens, even the ministry that God called us to can become a weight.

Recreational Activities: Do you know more about your favorite sports team than the Word of God? Do you know more about your favorite Hollywood star that the Word of God? Does your TV time outweigh your time spent with God? Do you invest more of your resources into temporal possessions and personal desires rather than in advancing the Kingdom of God? If so, then these things have become weights in our lives. We may need to re-prioritize.

> Wherefore seeing we also are compassed about with so great a cloud of witnesses, let us lay aside every weight, and the sin which so easily beset us, and let us run with patience the race that is set before us. (Hebrews 12:1)

The sin (which easily <u>beset us</u>; overwhelmed, weighed down): What is that one sin that the enemy always seem to be victorious over us? What is that one thing that we keep doing? It seems that we are delivered, then we find ourselves right back at the altar asking God to forgive us, again. As previously mentioned, the enemy knows what we like and how we like it. He may not tempt you with drinking alcohol or doing drugs because that's not your thing. He might not tempt you with robbing a bank or killing someone. But he may tempt you to commit adultery or fornication. He may tempt you to tell a lie or play the lottery. He may tempt you to prostitute your gift by using it just for financial gain. Let's take a look at this word sin to get a clearer understanding.

The word "sin" means to *miss the mark*. It is a term used by archers when they missed the target that they were aiming for. We miss the mark when we fail to be the person that God created us to be. We miss the mark when we fail to fulfill His plan for our lives. God has a specific plan for all of our lives, which is in alignment with His plan for the Kingdom. This is why He commands us to seek his Kingdom first.

> But seek ye first the kingdom of God, and his righteousness; and all these things shall be added unto you. (Matthew 6:33)

KING'DOM, n. [king and dom, jurisdiction.] *The territory or country that is subject to a king.* The Kingdom of God is the territory that is subject to God's authority. In a Kingdom, the king's authority goes beyond geographic region. The king's authority flows into all systems of the land: including governmental, educational, financial, social, etc. When we seek the Kingdom of God first, we are submitting to His will in every area of our lives. This will ensure that we are in alignment with His will and not missing the mark.

Other definitions of sin include, "lack of fellowship with God" (or anything that disturbs or disrupts this fellowship). Rejection of the truth or not being receptive to the Word of God is sin.

> For the wrath of God is revealed from heaven against all ungodliness and unrighteousness of men who <u>hold the truth in unrighteousness</u>. (Romans 1:18)

There are those who know the truth, but chose to live unrighteous. We must obey all of the Word (even those parts that we don't like). Sin is like a virus that does the damage to the body. The symptoms of the virus are the visible signs, but the root of sin is in the heart which cannot be seen. Sin is a progression that leads to death.

We must *hurry up* and get into position and wait to hear from God. Once the sin is removed from our lives and we are being the people who God created us to be, then we wait on our season of blessing.

> But they that wait upon the LORD shall renew *their* strength; they shall mount up with wings as eagles; they shall run, and not be weary; *and* they shall walk, and not faint.(Isaiah 40:31)

Abraham went *UP* into the mountain and waited on God to provide the sacrifice (Genesis 22:13). God cannot manifest Himself as Jehovah Jireh in most of our lives because we are not in the proper position. Moses went *UP* into the mountain to position himself to hear from God (Exodus 3:1-4). Joseph was taken *UP* out of the pit to become 2nd in command in Egypt (Gen 37:28). Our mindset must be elevated above our present circumstances. Many of us will remain in our PIT until we are renewed in our minds. Elijah sent his servant *UP* to the mountain to look for the cloud (I Kings 18:43). We may not receive the answer the first time, but we must stay in position. David looked *UP* to where his help came from (Psalm 121:1). Jesus said, "*and if I be lifted UP I will draw all men unto me*" (John 12:32). The Disciples were commanded to go to the Upper Room and wait for the promise (Acts 1:4). Let's not become impatient because we haven't seen some promises manifested in our lives. Let's hurry *up* and *wait* on the Lord.

> Be not deceived; God is not mocked: for whatsoever a man soweth, that shall he also reap. ^{8}For he that soweth to his flesh shall of the flesh reap corruption; but he that soweth to the Spirit shall of the Spirit reap life everlasting. ^{9}And let us not be weary in well doing: for in due season we shall reap, if we faint not. (Gal 6:7-9)

> I will stand upon my watch, and set me upon the tower, and will watch to see what he will say unto me, and what I shall answer when I am reproved. ^{2}And the Lord answered me, and said, Write the vision, and make it plain upon ta-

bles, that he may run that readeth it. [3]For the vision is yet for an appointed time, but at the end it shall speak, and not lie: though it tarry, wait for it; because it will surely come, it will not tarry. (Habakkuk 2:1-3)

9

A Lifestyle of Worship

> And Jesus answered him, The first of all the commandments is, Hear, O Israel; The Lord our God is one Lord: [30]And thou shalt love the Lord thy God with all thy heart, and with all thy soul, and with all thy mind, and with all thy strength: this is the first commandment. [31]And the second is like, namely this, Thou shalt love thy neighbour as thyself. There is none other commandment greater than these. (Mark 12:29-31, KJV)

There are many people who believe that worship is just an act that we do when we come into a corporate gathering on Sunday Mornings. While there is great value and importance in the corporate worship experience, there is more to worship than just "coming to church." We must learn as believers that our lives should demonstrate that we reverence God; that we love God; that we appreciate God; that we are surrendered to God. We must endeavor to demonstrate a "Lifestyle of Worship." We have learned throughout this book that worship is more than just singing a few songs. Becoming a True Worshiper will require us to go beyond the corporate worship experience. It requires us to do things that we probably wouldn't normally do. True Worship is extravagant love and extreme obedience. It requires us to give up some things that mean something to us. Worshipping God requires that we believe that God is who He says that He is and that He will do what He says he will do.

WORSHIP (World Dictionary Definition): Homage rendered to God, which it is sinful (idolatry) to render to any created being

- To show profound religious devotion and respect to; adore or venerate
- To be devoted to and full of admiration for
- To have or express feelings of profound adoration
- To attend services for worship (corporate gatherings)
- Admiring love or devotion

Hebrew Definition: shaw-khaw' to *prostrate* in homage to royalty or God: – bow (self) down, crouch, fall down (flat), humbly beseech, do (make) obeisance, do reverence, make to stoop, worship. Worship is the ability to magnify God with our heart, mind, body and spirit.

> And Jesus answered him, The first of all the commandments is, Hear, O Israel; The Lord our God is one Lord. (Mark 12:29)

We know that we are living in a time where people believe in all types of things. There are different religions, denominations, organizations, individuals, and principles, that people have based their faith on. Jesus said that there is only one true and living God. There are not many "gods" like the heathen nations were serving. This is the basis of our Christian faith! We believe what the Bible says and we hold to the fact that there is only one true and living God.

> Then saith Jesus unto him, Get thee hence, Satan: for it is written, Thou shalt worship the Lord thy God, and him only shalt thou serve. (Matthew 4:10)

> And thou shalt love the Lord thy God with all thy heart, and with all thy soul, and with all thy mind, and with all thy strength: this is the first commandment. (Mark 12:30)

We stated that one of the definitions of worship is "admiring love or devotion." To worship God is to love God. We demonstrate our love for God by obeying his Word. Thus to Truly Worship God is to obey the Word of God. John 14:15: "*If ye love me, keep my commandments.*" Living our lives in accordance with the Word of God is demonstrating a "Lifestyle of Worship". John 4:24: "*God is a Spirit: and they that worship him must worship him in spirit and in truth.*" We are commanded to love/worship God with our **ALL** (includes heart, soul, mind and strength) Heart: Kardia (kar-dee'-ah): the thoughts or feelings. It is appropriate to express emotions and feeling when we are worshiping God. Worship: To have or express feelings of profound adoration. Psalm 42:1: "*As the heart panteth after the water brooks, so panteth my soul after thee, O God.*" The deer is "panting" because he has been running. He wants to make it to the water brook to get refreshed. He knows that the water brook will cause the enemy who is chasing him to lose the scent. True Worshipers passionately seek God. True Worshipers thirst for God. True Worshipers are desperate to be in the presence of God. In God's presence is where we are refreshed and have protection.

During the course of our day, we encounter different situations that spark our emotions. (Love, anger, happiness, fear, sadness, trust, distrust, jealousy, etc.) We demonstrate a *lifestyle of worship* when we allow the Holy Spirit to lead us as we express our emotions. Ephesians 4:26: "*Be ye angry, and sin not: let not the sun go down upon your wrath.*"

> The LORD is my strength and my shield; my heart trusted in him, and I am helped: therefore my heart greatly rejoiceth; and with my song will I

praise him. (Psalm 28:7)

Soul: Psuche (psoo-khay'): *breath/spirit.* We are actually spirit beings that live in earthly bodies. When Adam was created, God "breathed" into him the "breath of life."

> And the LORD God formed man of the dust of the ground, and breathed into his nostrils the breath of life; and man became a living soul. (Genesis 2:7)

God "breathed" His spirit into us which is what produced life. When we love/worship God in spirit and in truth (in accordance with the Word), we are fulfilling God's intended purpose for creating man in the first place. God wanted a manifestation of Himself on the earth. He created us to look like him, act like Him, talk like Him, and even think like Him. When we live a *lifestyle of worship,* we are being who God created us to be.

> And thou shalt love the Lord thy God with all thy heart, and with all thy soul, and with all thy mind, and with all thy strength: this is the first commandment. (Mark 12:30)

Mind: Dianoia (dee-an'-oy-ah): *deep thought, imagination, mind, understanding.* We are commanded to love/worship God with our "understanding." The more we learn about God (attributes and characteristics) we can't help but to love/worship Him all the more. We must make a conscious effort to worship God with our lives. This doesn't happen by accident. We have to make an intelligent decision to be sold out to God by allowing Him to transform our minds.

> And be not conformed to this world: but be ye transformed by the renewing of your mind, that ye may prove what is that good, and acceptable, and perfect, will of God. (Romans 12:2)

When we live a lifestyle of worship, we properly manage our thought life. We don't allow the enemy to continue to dominate our minds and keep us in bondage (2 Corinthians 10:5). Casting down imaginations and every high thing that exalts itself against the knowledge of God, and bringing into captivity every thought to the obedience of Christ; True Worshipers line their thoughts up with the Word of God.

Thoughts (meditating of the Word) + Spoken Words (faith confessions) + Faith (cometh by hearing) + Action/Works = Manifested Miracles.

> And thou shalt love the Lord thy God with all thy heart, and with all thy soul, and with all thy mind, and with all thy strength: this is the first commandment. (Mark 12:30)

Strength: ischus (is-khoos') *ability, might, power, strength*. This can speak of loving/worshiping God with our "bodies."

> What? know ye not that your body is the temple of the Holy Ghost which is in you, which ye have of God, and ye are not your own? (1 Corinthians 6:19)

When we live a lifestyle of worship, we take care of our physical bodies. This includes eating healthy, regular exercise, taking safety precautions (i.e. driving safely, being vigilant and aware of our surroundings, etc.), vitamins and prescribed medications, etc. This can also speak of loving/worshiping God by going where He tells us to go and doing what he commands us to do. When we live a lifestyle of worship, we are loving/serving God with our ability. This speaks to the importance of being yourself and not trying to be someone else.

> For I say, through the grace given unto me, to every man that is among you, not to think of himself more highly than he ought to think; but to think soberly, according as God hath dealt to every man the measure of faith. (Romans 12:3, KJV)

> And the second is like, namely this, Thou shalt love thy neighbour as thyself. There is none other commandment greater than these. (Mark 12:31)

In Jesus' mind, a lifestyle of worship only included two commandments. Loving the Lord with all of our heart, soul, mind and strength. Love our neighbors as we love ourselves. One of the greatest demonstrations of a lifestyle of worship is the love that we show towards others (friends and enemies, saints and sinners). As we strive to *Become a True Worshiper*, let's look beyond the corporate gathering on Sunday mornings. While there is value and importance in the corporate worship experience, there is more to worship than just "coming to church." Let's let our lives demonstrate that we reverence God; that we love God; that we appreciate God; that we are surrendered to God. Let's endeavor to demonstrate a *lifestyle of worship*.

10

The Heart of a Servant

> Let this mind be in you, which was also in Christ Jesus: ⁶Who, being in the form of God, thought it not robbery to be equal with God: ⁷But made himself of no reputation, and took upon him the form of a servant, and was made in the likeness of men: ⁸And being found in fashion as a man, he humbled himself, and became obedient unto death, even the death of the cross. (Philippians 2:5-8)

As True Worshippers, it should be our sincere desire to want to display the image of Christ in our lives. Being that we were created in His image and after His likeness, we should be the direct reflection of who He is. When God sees us it should be as if He were looking into a mirror and the image that is reflected should be the image of His Son Jesus. What kind of person was the "man" Christ Jesus? What was the driving force that caused Him to impact the whole world? How can we be like Christ? Why did He say the things that He said or do the things that He did? What was always going through His mind? Lets take some time to focus on the Heart of a Servant. We are going to look at Jesus Christ and how He operated. We will also look at some other men in the Bible that were true servants who became mighty in the Kingdom of God.

There are several ways that the word "Servant" is translated in the scriptures. Let's focus on two of these words. The Hebrew word "*Ebed*" means being a slave not by choice. An example of this is when the Children of Israel were in bondage by the Egyptians. They were being held captive against their will. Another word for servant in the Hebrew language is the word "*Doulos*" which means being a slave by choice. It means being voluntary subject to the authority or will of another. To best describe this word, I will use another example. Let's say there were two slaves who married and began a family. Somehow, the man slave wins his freedom. He probably wouldn't want to leave his family, so he makes an arrangement with the slave owner to stay on as a bond slave (or doulos).

It was by choice that Jesus became a *servant*. For God so loved that He gave His only begotten Son. He offered of Himself and Jesus submitted to the authority of the Father's desire. Jesus did nothing of himself but was a true servant of God. He submitted to God who had the "rule" over Him.

> I can of mine own self do nothing: as I hear, I judge: and my judgment is just;

> because I seek not mine own will, but the will of the Father which hath sent me. (John 5:30)

Because of Christ's obedience in submitting to the authority (or will) of another, He was exalted.

> Wherefore God also hath highly exalted him, and given him a name which is above every name. (Philippians 2:9)

I think it is very important that True Worshippers, choir directors, praise & worship leaders, singers, dancers and musicians be members of the church where you are serving. Covenant relationship is very important. We should be submitted to a pastor who is going to pray for us, encourage us, rebuke us and provoke us to operate in excellence. Submission is a character trait that we must demonstrate if we are going to be like Christ. I know so many musicians who use their talent all over town and don't submit to anyone. I believe this leaves us vulnerable to the attacks of the enemy. We need a spiritual covering. We need to be held accountable. We need to submit. If Jesus took upon the form of a servant to do the will of His Father, so we are to take on the form of a servant to submit to our "spiritual leadership." We must be willing to submit to the authority that has been place over us.

> Obey them that have the rule over you, and submit yourselves: for they watch for your souls, as they that must give account, that they may do it with joy,

and not with grief: for that is unprofitable for you. (Hebrews 13:17)

There is a two-fold obligation in this passage of scripture. The followers must obey those who have the rule over them. This word in the Greek language is "Peitho" which is translated to agree, assure, believe, have confidence, be (wax) conflent, make friend, obey, persuade, trust, or to yield. It is important that we trust the God that is in our leaders. We must get to know their heart, their passions, their dislikes, their beliefs, etc. Not only should we know what they believe, we should obey and do those things that are commanded/demanded of us. Yield our members to the authority that is over us. The leaders also have an obligation in this scripture. They must watch for our souls. This requires sacrifice of themselves. They "watch" as if on duty for the attacks of the enemy.

> When the enemy shall come in like a flood, the Spirit of the Lord shall lift up a standard against him. (Isaiah 59:19)

To "Lift up a standard" means to put to flight. Just as a "watch" chases away any enemy that would try to invade the camp, so those that watch for our souls put to flight the enemies assigned to attack the Body. Our leaders must give account to God as to how we served the Body. They will have to give a report to God as to how well you served.

It would seem that all that I have been talking about is submission and taking a back seat to someone else. It would almost seem as if all the blessings are going to those in authority or who are leading. Let's look at a biblical principal that will change your life if you get a hold of it. Let's look into the lives of Elijah and Elisha and how God views the principal of servant hood.

> And when they had gone over, Elijah said to Elisha, Ask what I shall do for you before I am taken from you. And Elisha said, I pray you, let a <u>double portion of your spirit be upon me</u>. (2 Kings 2:9)

Let's first look at the life of Elijah so you will realize the magnitude of what Elisha was asking for. Elijah the Prophet came out of nowhere and declared that it would not rain until he said that it would (and the skies dried up). God sustained him by feeding him miraculously: Ravens brought him food in the morning and the evening everyday. God instructed him to dwell with a widow woman and her son and sustained them during the drought. This woman's son died and Elijah raised him from the dead. Elijah had a show down with the 450 false prophets in which he called down fire from heaven. He went into hiding at the threats of Jezebel. He thought that he was the only true prophet left in Israel. Even great men of God get discouraged sometimes. This is why it is very important to continually pray for our leadership and keep them encouraged. Elijah goes into the cleft of a mountain and God passed by in a wind, then an earthquake, then a fire, but Elijah was not moved. It was then that God spoke to him in a still small voice. Elijah recognized the voice of the Lord and reverenced the Presence of God (wrapped his face in his mantle). It was at this point that God instructed him to anoint this young man Elisha to be a prophet.

> And Jehu the son of Nimshi shalt thou anoint to be king over Israel: and Elisha the son of Shaphat of Abelmeholah shalt thou anoint to be prophet in thy room. (1 Kings 19:16)

Let's identify some character traits of Elisha. Why did God hand pick him to follow one of the greatest prophets of all times.

> So he departed thence, and **found Elisha** the son of Shaphat, **who was plowing** with twelve yoke of oxen before him, and he with the twelfth: and Elijah passed by him, and cast his mantle upon him. [20]And he left the oxen, and ran after Elijah, and said, Let me, I pray thee, kiss my father and my mother, and then I will follow thee. And he said unto him, Go back again: for what have I done to thee? [21]And he returned back from him, and took a yoke of oxen, and slew them, and boiled their flesh with the instruments of the oxen, and

> gave unto the people, and they did eat. Then he arose, and went after Elijah, and ministered unto him. (1 Kings 19:19-21)

Elisha was found working. God chooses people who are not lazy and not afraid to work/people who are not slothful. Elisha was receptive to the call of God from the Man of God. Elisha left all that he knew (his way of life) to follow the Man of God (remember the word doulos?). God may be calling us to re-prioritize some things in our lives to line up with His will for our lives. Elisha ministered to Elijah. He was a servant to the man of God. He washed Elijah's hands and did all of those menial tasks that made many people laugh at him. As true servants, there are those that won't understand Kingdom principles and will ridicule you, scorn you and call you crazy. You must hold fast to your profession of faith and make your calling and election sure.

Elijah tested Elisha's servant-hood on several occasions. 2 Kings 2:1-6 (Trip to Bethel, Jericho and Jordan). Elisha stayed on his post. Elijah and Elisha understood the principle of having a servant's heart. Elisha didn't lose out on anything by serving the Man of God. As True Worshippers, we must master being followers if we ever want to be great leaders. We must submit ourselves to our leadership and trust that God will elevate us in due season. As we submit to those over us we must get their spirit. Elisha didn't ask for a double portion of God's Spirit, he asked for a double portion of Elijah's spirit (knowing that Elijah was empowered by God). David also understood this principle and duplicated warriors that were just like him. David was a giant killer and he produced giant killers.

- Adino: slew 800 men with a spear in one battle
- Eleazar: fought so hard with David that his hand clung to his sword
- Shammah: defended a ground full of lentles
- Benaiah: killed a lion, in a pit, on a snowy day.

These men were ordinary men who did extraordinary things because they tapped into the anointing that was on their leader. They served the man of God with out reservation and received all of the spoils and blessings that David received. True Worshippers, if we really want to see the blessings of God flow in our lives and ministries we must develop the heart of a servant. We are not greater that our Lord Jesus Christ. If He became a servant for us, how much more should we become servants for Him.

11

Preparing the Way for Your Ministry

True Worshippers, I know that we are anointed, gifted, talented, called and needed in our local churches. We may even have international calls on our lives and minister throughout the world. Sometimes, the demand on the anointing on our lives can cause us to loose focus on what this thing is really all about. We must always keep God first. Always remember that God doesn't need us to be who He is; we need Him to be who we are. With that being said, it must be understood that God does need us to be an extension of Him here on earth, working on His behalf. It was because of the obedience of one man that Jesus was properly introduced to the world. I believe that God will speak to our hearts as He uncovers some principles that most of us already know, but may need rekindling. Today we are going to talk a little about John the Baptist.

> Now when John had heard in the prison the works of Christ, he sent two his disciples, [3] And said to him, Art thou

he that should come or do we look for another. (Matthew 11:2-3)

Let's look at John's life and try to figure what was going on with him that would seem to make him lose focus and question his faith. It was not a coincidence that the birth of John was announced 6 months before Jesus' birth. His ministry was the forerunner to Christ's ministry. It was John who baptized Jesus prior to Jesus beginning His public ministry. In many aspects, John was a very important part of Jesus' life. Since John's parents were of the priestly line of Aaron (Luke 1:5), so was he—though he himself did not become a priest. Instead, he became much more! Undoubtedly, his parents helped to mold him to be the unique person he became. Dedicated to God's service from birth, he was to drink no wine or strong drink. He would be filled with the Holy Spirit from birth (Luke 1:15). His parents were promised that he would be called "the prophet of the Highest" and that he would "go before the face of the Lord to prepare his ways" (Luke 1:76). John lived in the wilderness area of Judea until he appeared in his special role to prepare the hearts of the people for the Messiah and His kingdom. John's whole personality and his vocabulary reflected the desert lifestyle. He was fully equipped for his ministry and drew many of his preaching illustrations from that desert experience.

John's parents were Zacharias (a priest) and Elisabeth. Both were righteous and walking in the commandments of the Lord (Luke 1:6). The Bible says that they were blameless. Not only did they have a good report with God, but with men. Both were old (beyond childbearing age) and Elisabeth was barren. Zacharias was faithful in is duties as a minister in the Lord's house. It was his turn to burn incense in the temple (there was a multitude of people praying as Zacharias burned the incense). The angel Gabriel appeared to him as he was performing his duties

Here we have an ordinary man, performing his ordinary tasks and received a divine visitation and blessing from God. Note two things that were going on: Everyone was in their position (VERY IMPORTANT) and it was God's appointed time to manifest the promise.

> I will stand upon my watch, and set me upon the tower, and will watch and see what he will say unto me, and what shall I answer when I am reproved. ²And the Lord answered me, and said, Write the vision, make it plain upon tables, that he may run that readeth it. **³ For the vision is yet for an appointed time**, but at the end it shall speak, and not lie: though it tarry, wait for it; Because it will surely come, it will not tarry. (Habakkuk 2:1-3)

God manifests His power and performs miracles when things are in order. God sent a word, after not speaking for 400 years, to an ordinary man who had a good report and obeyed the commandments of the Lord. Zacharias wasn't perfect, but he was surrendered to the purpose and plan of God. There were prophecies/promises that had to be fulfilled.

Some of us have been faithful and committed to God's word and doing his work, and He is going to birth those things that we have committed to Him. Even though it may look like we are barren, and old, and beyond our years; and there may have even been a drought where we didn't think God was speaking. He is getting ready to birth some Johns in our lives. John (forerunner) preceded Jesus (the Anointed one). John (prepared) made way for the blessing (Jesus).

We must start looking for the ***forerunners*** for our blessing (i.e. Getting a passport, opening saving accounts, prepare yourself to be blessed, etc.). John was not only a miracle child, but he was a blessing to his family and impacted the world around him. He was filled with the Holy Ghost from his mother's womb. His mother was filled with the Holy Ghost (Luke 1:28) and his father was filled with the Holy Ghost (Luke 1:67). He changed the way that the word was being preached. No one else was doing it like he did it:

> Now when John had heard in the prison the works of Christ, he sent two his disciples, ³ And said to him, Art thou he that should come or do we look for another. (Matt 11:2-3)

As we look at the passage of scripture, we see that John was now in prison and was soon to be executed. This mighty warrior had spent his entire life preaching the "Kingdom of Heaven is at hand," and now it would seem here as if he is questioning everything that he believed. I personally don't think this was a matter of John questioning his faith. He was too sold out to question his faith now. Based on the way the Religious Leaders lived back then, he probably knew that eventually they would come for him. I think John was wanting reassurance that he had not spent his entire life and all of his energy for nothing. "I just want to know before I leave this earth that I was in the presence of the True and Living God. I want to know that the Promise was delivered in my life time." (Heb 11:39-40)

What has God promised you? What are some of the things that you want to see during your lifetime? Is it the salvation of loved ones? Is it financial? Ministry? John had positioned himself and dedicated himself to a position where he could ask the question. "Is this the blessing that I have been looking for?" We must position ourselves and dedicate our lives to the purpose of God

> Now when John had heard in the prison the works of Christ, he sent two his disciples, ³ And said to him, Art thou he that should come or do we look for another. ⁴ Jesus answered and said unto them, Go and shew John again those things which ye do hear and see. ⁵The

> blind receive their sight, and the lame walk, the leepers are cleansed, and the deaf hear, the dead are raised up, and the poor have the gospel preached unto them. ⁶ And blessed is he, whosoever shall not be offended in me. (Matt 11:2-6)

Jesus sent back word to John saying, "Look at the evidence, John. What do you see? Based on your study of the scriptures and the reports of the events that are taking place, what do you think?" **Start looking for evidence of the promises of God**. If we are being obedient to His Word we should start seeing some results. We should not still be in the same place where we first believed. Jesus says that there never has been another like John. What a testimony coming from Jesus. Jesus didn't rebuke John and called him "oh ye of little faith." He knew who John was. He knew what John had done and why he did it. John preceded Jesus so that the world was prepared for Jesus. Jesus was born to die. John preceded Jesus in birth, ministry and death.

Let us be forerunners for the next blessing in our world. Let's prepare the way for the coming of the Lord. We must birth those ministries that are going to change mindsets and the way people do things. We must establish kingdom principles that will make a way for the King of Glory to return.

Conclusion

It is my prayer that this book blesses the life of everyone who reads it. Whether you are a senior pastor, minister of music, choir director, singer, musician, or True Worshipper, I believe that God expects us to invest in our ministries. God took of His divine nature and deposited seeds of greatness in us. He expects us to water that seed in order to manifest that greatness. It doesn't matter what our calling, gift, talent or ministry is. The important thing is that we be the people who God created us to be. I have over 30 years of experience in the music ministry department and God has taught me a few things over the years. I am ever learning and striving to manifest more of the greatness that God has deposited into me. My goal is to provide some wisdom, insight and guidance to someone else so that they don't make some of the mistakes that I have made. My prayer is that the words of this book assist someone in achieving the greatness that God has deposited in them.

I speak the blessing of God into your life. I declare that you are who God says that you are and that you can do what God says that you can do. I speak the favor of God over your life and ministry. I declare that you are walking in excellence of character and manifesting the Kingdom of God everywhere that you go. I decree that the ministry that is inside of you is destroying the kingdom of darkness. I declare that you will submit to your senior pastor and be faithful to the place that God has called you to serve. I declare that you will commit to the development of your gifts and will commit to developing those who serve with you. I speak that you will honor God with your gifts, your substance, and most importantly your life! I declare and decree that you are a True Worshipper!

In Jesus' name, Amen.

About the Author

Timothy D. Lucas is the Senior Pastor of Kingdom Outreach Ministries International located in Dumfries, Virginia. He is married to his bride of 20 years, First Lady Rochelle Lucas. Together, they have three beautiful children (Kimyata, Cherelle and Tim Jr.). Pastor Lucas is recently retired from the United States Marine Corps as a First Sergeant after serving 21 years of honorable service. Pastor Lucas has served in various areas of ministry in the church throughout the years; which include Assistant Pastor, Minister of Music, Worship Leader, Choir Director, President of Men's Department, Sunday School Director/Teacher, and Youth Leader. Pastor Lucas acknowledged his call to preach the gospel in 1998 and was licensed and Ordained as an Elder by Pastor Elmer Ross, Senior Pastor of Fresh Anointing World Christian Center.

Being a United States Marine, Pastor Lucas has been blessed to have traveled throughout the world. He has planted himself everywhere that he has been and has allowed the Lord to bless him, as well as be a blessing to the ministries that he has served. While stationed on Okinawa Japan, Pastor Lucas and his family joined Kingdom Outreach Ministries International (KOMI) - Okinawa. It was there that God connected them to Pastor Joseph W. King and Evangelist Kimberly King. This union would prove to be God-ordained as well as prophetic. They began working together to advance the Kingdom of God throughout the island of Okinawa. As Pastor Lucas embraced the vision of KOMI and served faithfully as Assistant Pastor, Minister of Music and several other key positions in the ministry, Pastor King noticed the greater call that was on his life. When the time came to leave Okinawa, Pastor Lucas was sent to plant a ministry in Virginia. The call was accepted and Kingdom Outreach Ministries International -Virginia was established.

Pastor Lucas is continually seeking God and yielding to the leading of the Holy Spirit as God is bringing the vision to pass. The mission is to Reach a Diverse Community, Perfect the Saints, and Impact the World.

Pastor Lucas is a powerful motivational speaker, preacher/teacher, writer and musician. He is available to conduct seminars, workshops, revivals, etc. to teach and assist your congregations, worship teams, and musicians how to become True Worshippers!

Booking Information for Speaking/Preaching Engagements:

P.O. Box 618
Triangle, Virginia 22172

Email: timothy.lucas@komivirginia.com
Phone: 703-221-3599
Church Website: www.komivirginia.com

Made in the USA
Middletown, DE
01 May 2015